SHAMANIC LEADERSHIP

Authentic Strategy and Service Beyond Performance

ANGEL GOLD

FEATURING: JORGE LUIS DELGADO · LAURA DI FRANCO
SHARLA DUNCAN · RACHELLE GOLDING
ELIZA JAMES · APRIL KAISER · DUSTIN KAISER
GRACE KOHN · SPENCER MACDONALD · EMOKE MOLNAR
DAPHNE PARAS · KRISTINA SKYE · GRACE SOLARIS
BRADFORD W. TILDEN · ATLANTIS WOLF

"Angel Gold has put together a compendium of explorations that will take you on a wild and inspirational journey, a deep dive into the revelations and insights that can come from a willingness to open yourself to Spirit and provide guidance for your soul's path."

~ Dr. Steven Farmer, Psychotherapist, Shamanic Practitioner, and Bestselling Author of Earth Magic and *Animal Spirit Guides*

*

"In a world faced with what seems like insurmountable change, an entirely new form of leadership is required. You'll find the innovation and inspiration you need in *Shamanic Leadership*. Angel Gold has tenderly and skillfully compelled you to consider a rich, purpose-driven, deeply potent form of leadership – the kind of leadership that emerges from the fearless yet vulnerable exploration of your own soul. Commit yourself to this medicine, and you'll not only heal yourself, but you will also lead the world to healing!"

~Dr. Ahriana Platten, Bestselling Author of *Rites and Rituals: Harnessing the Power of Sacred Ceremony*

*

"I am so honored to have walked with you on your path, Angel. As you know, I do not believe in coincidence, and I know it was simply what was required to move forward. The team still talks about all the amazing experiences, growth, and learning we had because of your time with us. Thank you for continuing to bring the light!"

~ Dr. Raeleen Manjak, DM/OL, ΔMΔ, CPHR

*

"*Shamanic Leadership* is a gift and sacred longing answered. Powerful stories and words that weave wisdom from the embodied feminine and masculine leadership emerging in the world today."

~ Stephanie Urbina Jones, #1 Billboard Country Music Songwriter, Dreamer, Artist of Life

Shamanic Leadership

Authentic Strategy and Service Beyond Performance

Angel Gold

FEATURING: JORGE LUIS DELGADO · LAURA DI FRANCO
SHARLA DUNCAN · RACHELLE GOLDING
ELIZA JAMES · APRIL KAISER · DUSTIN KAISER
GRACE KOHN · SPENCER MACDONALD · EMOKE MOLNAR
DAPHNE PARAS · KRISTINA SKYE · GRACE SOLARIS
BRADFORD W. TILDEN · ATLANTIS WOLF

DISCLAIMER

This book is designed to provide competent, reliable, and educational information on community and business building, as well as other related subject matter. However, it is sold with the understanding that the authors and publisher specifically disclaim all responsibility for any liability, loss, or risk, personal or otherwise, incurred as a consequence, directly or indirectly, of the use and application of any of the contents of this publication.

In order to maintain the anonymity of others, the names and identifying characteristics of some people, places, and organizations described in this book have been changed.

This publication contains content that may be potentially triggering or disturbing. Individuals who are sensitive to certain themes are advised to exercise caution while reading.

The opinions, ideas, and recommendations contained in this publication do not necessarily represent those of the publisher. The use of any information provided in this book is solely at your own risk.

Our authors represent cultures worldwide, and as such, there may be differences in language and expressions. As a global publisher, we have made the conscious choice not to edit these nuances, so each chapter is authentic and in its author's words.

Know that the experts here have shared their tools, practices, and knowledge with you with a sincere and generous intent to assist you on your personal journey. Please contact them with any questions you may have about the techniques or information they provided. They will be happy to assist you further and be an ongoing resource for your success!

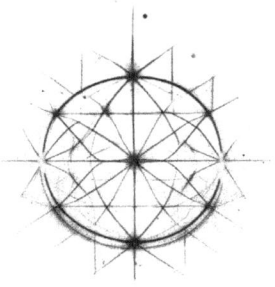

INVOCATION

Unmasking Human Domestication
Angel Gold

Birth is not entry onto Earth,

it is assignment

into a dream already woven.

To be born into this world is to enter a dream already dreamed.

From the moment we draw breath, the cords of domestication begin to wrap around us. Our families, religions, governments, and cultures hand us their books of law, carved from fear and control, and we're told this is life.

To belong, we must obey.

To be loved, we must betray some essential piece of our wild, original self.

This is the Toltec inheritance we speak of: the dream of the planet. A dream that trains us to forget our inherent divinity and trade our freedom for acceptance. A dream that convinces us who we are isn't enough, and so we must perform, achieve, prove, and strive.

But beneath the noise, another current moves; the old medicine.

It's the memory of a time when leadership meant walking in right relationship with the Earth, with the unseen, and with one another, when service was not performance but devotion, and when strategy wasn't manipulation, but alignment with the living intelligence of creation itself.

The shamanic path doesn't offer comfort, nor does it promise success as the world measures it. Instead, it strips away the lies, breaks the agreements that keep us small, and burns down the false altars of productivity and perfection so we can stand bare again—sovereign, luminous, and true.

Shamanic Leadership is a remembering.

Not of how to lead in the old ways, but how to return to the original agreement: that we came here as sparks of the infinite, bytes of light, carrying medicine only we can carry. That our work in the world is not to prove, but to embody, not to perform, but to serve.

This book is an initiation.

It won't flatter you.

It won't let you hide behind borrowed masks.

It will invite you into the fire where the performer dies and the leader is born.

If you're reading these words, you already know something is stirring.

You've heard the whisper: *There must be another way.*

You're right.

There is.

But it's not found in the rules of the world of man.

It rises from within as you reclaim the wild, untamed truth that has been waiting beneath your skin all along.

Here begins your passage—from domestication into sovereignty, from performance into presence.

From exile into homecoming.

To belong, we obey.
To be loved, we betray.
Piece by piece, our feral strips away;
Soul remembers, find your way.
Through the bugs and the bees
Through the flowers and the trees
It's the Shaman's way
Aligned to stay

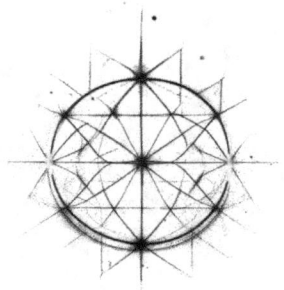

NOTE TO YOU COURAGEOUS READERS ASCENSION SYMPTOMS ARE A THING

So, you pick up this book and binge the whole thing and are now finding yourself setting up camp in the bathroom because your body is going through a full detox in unimaginable ways, and you don't know what the hell is happening!

WELCOME TO THE ASCENSION DETOX CLUB

The common Canadian phrase, "Does a bear shit in the woods?" became a reality in my world after an intense power journey in Teotihuacan, Mexico, as I made my way home and had to drive through the Rocky Mountains with no bathrooms along the highway. If you want full, glorious details with lots of laughs, head over to our Bytes of Light Podcast and watch Episode 4.

Nobody escapes unscathed. The cool thing is that everyone experiences ascension symptoms differently, as we all came onto this planet with different ancestral programming. I can provide you with a list of things that may happen, so you are aware. If these things are happening to you, know it's an integral part of the process.

Physically, our body holds cellular memory. When we choose to shift habits, patterns, and own our wounds and stories, our bodies will act physically as if in danger, they are sick, or feel like they will die.

NOTICE, I SAY OUR BODIES ACT THAT WAY

We are choosing to shift our attention and awareness so our conscious brains understand we are willingly choosing to go on this ride. This does not mean our bodies will be able to keep up with the rate we are loading light into our systems.

Bingeing this book would be the same as sitting out in the direct sun with no sunscreen or shade. It would amount to incoming burns and heat stroke for some, while others may be simply fine. It all depends on your level of awareness and whether some of the stories trigger you or not. The level of commitment you bring to your own personal growth will correlate with your level of ascension and the number of symptoms you experience. Slow and steady, always stay with yourself and honor where you are at in every moment. Self-care is your best friend!

IT TAKES THE ENERGY OF A WARRIOR TO SHIFT OUR CONSCIOUSNESS INTO THE LIGHT

Know we all are honored by you reading our permeated words of light and are here for you when you have questions or want more information. You are never alone on this journey.

On Angel's website, you will find online courses and one-on-one packages to assist you in furthering your elevation and awareness. You can start by allowing the ascension symptoms to guide you as you get started.

For the ascension symptoms guideline, follow this link:
https://www.skool.com/fire-heart-mystery-school/classroom

Stardust falls from the sky,
I'm sitting on the moon
I hear the call from humanity,
I know I must go soon

Growling as my paws Land on
earthen floor Fur and claws
Fangs and blood,
Gaia welcomes me to the hood

Where are you?
I see you up in blue Howling,
the lonely Call of the Wolf
My soul calls out to you

Stillness, darkness,
must find my vision.
Severing throats of those
on a dark mission

Why am I here?
What does my soul crave this time?
My new furry soul basket
Lets out a small whine

As I look into the stars and ask for a sign.
"Remember who you are, little one,
this next trip to Earth
I promise, will be divine."

Nestling in my den Among my
brethren Protected and held while
I heal deep within

The sacred Feminine
This is my medicine
Medicine of the Wolf

-WILLOW WHITE WOLF

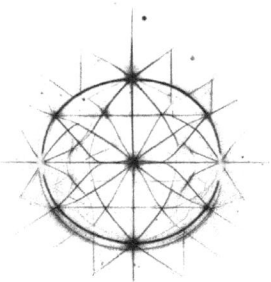

DREAMING WITH WILLOW WHITE WOLF

I vividly remember taking my beautiful white husky for a walk daily as a child. Children will categorize things they learn in the structures they have already been domesticated with, and in my tiny little world, this imaginary pet I had was indeed a dog.

Most humans I've conversed with in this world had imaginary human friends. Mine showed up in fur form, and my earliest remembrance was of this huge, beautiful, white dog.

Walking down the sidewalk with my hand resting on the powerful shoulder blades of this magnificent creature, for me, it was as real as the sun shining on my face.

It was not until I was in my teens that I saw a picture of a white wolf and made the connection; my dog was not a husky. It was a wolf. This realization opened magical portals of possibilities I chose to go down. How did I know what a wolf looked like as a small child, without ever seeing one? This question had me seeking answers that the humans surrounding me did not have.

When you ask the Universe to show you signs, they show up in ways you do not see coming, and in 2013, a human showed up in my world with deep wolf medicine to share.

I was facilitating at a private drug and alcohol retreat center, nestled in the Kootenay mountains, where part of the medicine is a weekly sweat lodge on an indigenous reserve with its elders. This man had an experience where he could not breathe through the intense heat and was about to ask to leave the lodge when a wolf curled up to his chest and breathed cool air into his mouth as she lay with him. Upon telling this experience to me, he shared that he had been raising two wolf cubs from eight weeks old, and they were a year old now. The little female, Willow, came to him in the sweat lodge.

A month later, he took me to another province where the wolves were being cared for, only to discover they were both shot and killed for their pelts during that brief time he was away in recovery by the indigenous on the reserve next to them.

The ruthless realization hit like an atomic bomb. Willow was already dead when she came to visit him in the sweat lodge. River, on the other hand, ran after he witnessed his sister being killed. He covered hundreds of kilometers before being shot in a farmer's field and ending his journey on Earth this round as well.

With my attunement to wolf medicine and his experience with these baby wolves' short lives, we chose to take on their names in honor of their impactful journey in our lives, and Willow White Wolf was born within.

Wolves mate for life.

After half a dozen years, when one partner chooses a different life and kills the storyline, how does the other move on?

How does the whole pack move on without the alpha male? Oh wait.

Are 'alpha' and 'male' the only two words that go together? What about alpha female?

What does alpha mean?

What is the opposite, and where do I fit into the mix?

As a human with a female soul basket?

These questions had me digging into the depths of my soul for this last decade. *Who am I, and how do I want to show up in this world at this unprecedented time on earth?*

We are experiencing a quantum shift on this planet, where the patriarchal ways are being dismantled as Mama Gaia says "no" to some of the behaviors happening here on Earth. We are all being asked to look internally and challenge the agreements we have been domesticated with, and make better, more informed choices moving forward.

But how? We know things need to change, both internally and externally.

The question is, where do we start?

In my Toltec Shamanic apprenticeship, we spent years unraveling the concepts of 'power over versus power within' and the subtleties of control and manipulation within relationships. This has been great medicine as the world experiences the shift of us humans leaning more into the divine feminine aspects of who we are and what that looks like.

As I experimented with these energies, it became clear I was born with a generous capacity to feel and see subtle energies; however, those abilities were suppressed by my environment and lack of knowledge as a child. The divine masculine within me prevailed, and I made my way through life with a warrior's heart, choosing leadership as my form of communication and community.

As I delved deeper into the underworld, the shadow aspect of myself and my ancestral lineage, I surrendered to the goddess within, forgiving myself for all the mistakes I had made along this journey, forgiving those who had harmed me, and vowed to listen more deeply to my soul, knowing there was more medicine within. Three years ago, I committed to the Ruiz family in an intense apprenticeship and gave them permission to 'train Willow.' This feral aspect inside me was full of fire, which I had no control over, and she needed puppy training.

She had been hurt, abused, abandoned, and almost killed. She needed help, and to heal her, I had to ask my warrior to put her sword down, surrender, forget all I had known, and allow these healers to assess and give me the experiences I needed to awaken the goddess within.

Three men. What a concept. How did these men teach me the goddess way?

Energetic agility is the secret sauce
to keep authenticity alive in modernized gender roles.

Agility means you are skilled in both alpha and omega, and can pivot between the two embodiments at will, choosing whichever best serves the moment.

Rather than seeing these aspects as something fixed, you see them as a dance that occurs from moment to moment, each partner feeling into the situation and deciding which aspect to offer based on what would best serve the moment.

To train yourself to move between alpha and omega takes practice, no doubt, and in my experience, I needed healers who could "out alpha me" so I could lean in and strengthen my goddess spiritual muscles, knowing I was safe and held.

It takes advanced awareness to know which aspect you are occupying and what is needed within the relationship in question. This is where true, authentic leadership is born. You can only teach to the level of what you embody on both sides.

It takes practice to master the capacity to switch aspects on the fly.

My wish for humanity is to understand this sacred dance of the divine feminine and masculine aspects within. Ignite the passion for oneness by diving into your own heart to discover you truly are the love of your life. You can create your own safety, be your own warrior, as well as nurture the creative oracle that births magic into this world. We are both; we house both and all things. Our energy connects to all things on this planet because we are all one.

As you start to embody these energies and heighten your awareness, humans who can match and dance this agile dance will also start to show up in your world to play with. That, my loves, is why we are here!

Let us dive into the mystery together and allow our puppies to play!

Table of Contents

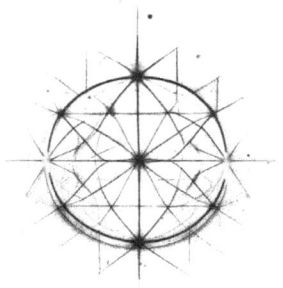

INTRODUCTION

WOLF MEDICINE

The Embodied Way of Leadership
Angel Gold

Wolf of the wild, wolf of the dream,
Wolf who carries the Starfire of Sirius in your eyes, teach us.

Teach us to howl when the night is long.
Teach us to listen when the wind speaks.
Teach us to stand alone in the wilderness,
and to merge with our pack when the time is right.

We call you now as guide and as mirror.
May your medicine re-weave our understanding of leadership,

beyond performance, beyond domination,
into the fierce and tender truth of what it means to serve.

THE DISTORTION OF LEADERSHIP

In the dream of the West, we've mistaken the spotlight for sovereignty. Leadership is sold to us in costumes of rank, performance, and power-over. The one with the title, the one with the crown, the one on the screen, we name them "leader."

But too often, those who wear these mantles have not yet met themselves in the dark.

They may command attention, but they don't cultivate presence.

They may demand obedience, but they can't inspire devotion.

They learn to wear a mask and pretend, but have no intention of changing their manipulative ways.

Authority isn't leadership.

Management isn't leadership.

Control isn't leadership.

True leadership is a frequency, not a function.

It's not inherited, bought, or assigned. It's born from alignment. It radiates from integrity. It transmits through energy before a single word is spoken.

And so, we turn to wolf, who remembers what we forgot.

WOLF AS WAY-SHOWER

Across cultures, wolves have been revered as teachers and pathfinders.

- In Native traditions, wolf is the embodiment of intuition, the one who walks between the worlds and brings guidance from the unseen.

- In Celtic lore, wolf is a guardian of thresholds, guiding souls through death and rebirth.

- In star medicine, wolf carries the codes of Sirius, the blazing star whose wisdom has long been a compass for humanity.

To walk with wolves is to remember how to navigate both earth and sky, both instinct and vision. Wolf medicine teaches us leadership isn't about performance but about presence, not domination but devotion.

Wolves don't lead by force, they lead by resonance. The pack follows because it feels the integrity of the one out front, not because it's coerced.

WILDNESS AND FEARLESSNESS

As we observe the wolf, we see and admire its wildness and fearlessness. And yet, these are the very qualities most humans fear, for wolf mirrors back the feral nature we learn to suppress. Society programs us to be "civilized," to tame our instincts, to bury our hunger. But beneath the conditioning, we remain animals with wild spirits still drumming in our bones.

To access true, authentic power, we must remember our own wildness. We must risk being misunderstood, feared, or judged to reclaim that instinctual part of ourselves. Wolf shows us how. By daring to be unapologetically wild, the wolf teaches us to take risks, face our deepest fears, and trust the higher self that whispers direction.

THE SOLITARY AND THE PACK

There are seasons when the lone wolf path calls us. These are not times of exile, but of initiation. Alone in the wilderness, stripped of distraction, we learn to access our channel, connect to the divine current that flows through all life, and trust our own intuition's voice. This solitude strengthens us, refines us, and prepares us.

And then there are seasons when the pack is everything. Wolves love to be social, to share hunts, to raise pups together, to howl beneath the same moon. They even mate for life, proving devotion and loyalty aren't human inventions, but wild truths. Yes, puppy love is real!

Wolf medicine shows us that true mastery lies in balancing both solitude and community. Too much isolation breeds spirit starvation. Too much merging dissolves individuality. But when we weave the two, we find strength that's both sovereign and communal.

With that balance, the pack becomes a wave of transformation.

Together, wolves can enter unfamiliar territory, set new intent for the whole, and become pathfinders of evolution.

This is leadership: the ability to move as one without erasing the many.

THE TRUTH OF ALPHA

In Western imagination, "alpha" has been twisted into a caricature of dominance: the loudest voice, the strongest fist, the conqueror. But in wolf medicine, alpha isn't a tyrant but a servant.

The alpha leads for the good of the pack. They carry the responsibility of protection, guidance, and provision. Their authority isn't seized, but earned, and when another wolf rises with greater strength or vision, the old alpha yields with dignity, knowing their value remains. They don't vanish; they shift roles. In wolf culture, leadership is fluid. Authority exists only to serve the whole.

This is a radical teaching for humanity: leadership isn't about clinging to power, but about stewarding it with humility. Leadership is love made visible through service.

A STORY OF ABANDONMENT AND REMEMBERING

There was a time in my life when I gave my power away.

He carried the confidence of a man born into a culture that crowned him leader before he earned it. He wore the mask of wisdom, strength, and protector. And I, longing for partnership, safety, and for someone to share the weight, handed him my trust.

At first, it seemed easier to follow. I accepted the minimum breadcrumbs of relational service. He spoke with authority, moved with speed and certainty, and wrapped his words in conviction.

He believed in his own performance. And for a time, I did, too.

But the mask began to slip.

His leadership wasn't rooted in service or presence; it was rooted in control and dominance, in privilege, in the illusion that to command was to lead. He wielded his power to control, silence, and bend and manipulate to his own agenda. And under the weight of it, something in me collapsed.

This is how domestication works. You mute your instincts. You abandon your wildness to keep the peace, stay safe, and belong. In doing so, I lost my way.

I gave up ground that was never his to take.

And it almost cost me my life.

My body broke beneath the strain. My spirit ached from betrayal. Not only his betrayal, but my betrayal of myself. I allowed someone to stand where wolf was meant to stand in me.

And yet, even in the darkest nights, wolf didn't leave.

I felt her presence, a low growl at the base of my spine, a howl threading its way through my dreams, a glimmer of Sirius reminding me:

You are not prey. You are pack. You are leader.

Wolf's medicine is reclamation. And so, I reclaimed.

I stepped away from the shadow of false leadership, from the illusion that domination is strength.

I walked back into my wilderness.

I pressed my feet to the Earth,

listened to the rhythm of my own heartbeat as drum,

and called my spirit back from the places I abandoned it.

And there I remembered: True leadership isn't the mask of certainty.

It's the willingness to walk with integrity, to balance the alpha and the omega within, and to embody both the feral wildness of instinct and the tender devotion of care.

Wolf taught me that leadership isn't something to outsource or something to hand away. It begins in my own body, in my own breath, in my willingness to stand sovereign and to walk with others in mutual respect.

That near-death season became initiation.

The wound became a vow:

- Never again would I mistake performance for presence.

- Never again would I follow a mask.

- I would walk only with those who faced their own wilderness and returned with medicine to share.

- I will never again partner with someone who isn't devoted to me, for leadership and love alike must be rooted in devotion. Anything less isn't partnership but pretense.

- And I would lead not by dominance, but by resonance. Not by control, but by awakening.

BALANCING MASCULINE AND FEMININE

For centuries, the West has been dominated by wounded masculine energy—relentless doing, conquering, controlling. This imbalance birthed division, hostility, and exploitation.

Wolf medicine calls us back to balance.

Masculine energy, in its essence, is clarity, direction, and action. Feminine energy is intuition, creativity, and compassion.

Wolf embodies both the sharp precision of the hunt and the tender devotion of raising pups: the howl that pierces the night and the nuzzle of affection within the den.

To embody wolf medicine in leadership is to weave these polarities within ourselves, to lead with both strength and softness, to act with both decisiveness and listening, and to create spaces where clarity and compassion walk hand-in-hand.

This balance isn't theoretical; it's embodied. You feel it in the presence of a true leader: firm yet open, fierce yet tender, decisive yet receptive. This is what humanity starves for.

PRACTICE

Wolf medicine isn't an idea to admire; it's a way to embody.

- The Lone Wolf Practice: Take a day each month to wander alone. Leave behind devices, roles, and expectations. Let yourself listen deeply to your own inner howl.

- The Pack Practice: Gather your circle. Share food, stories, and silence. Notice how each member carries medicine for the whole. Honor it. Speak it aloud.

- Alpha and Omega Balance: In moments of decision, pause. Ask: Am I acting from domination, or from service? Am I balancing clarity with compassion, doing with listening? Adjust until the two currents move together.

These simple practices, lived over time, shift leadership from performance to presence.

CLOSING INVOCATION

Wolf medicine isn't outside you. It lives in your marrow, in your heartbeat, in the part of you that refuses to be domesticated.

You're both lone wolf and pack. You're both howl and silence. You're both alpha and omega.

To lead isn't to command; it's to remember. To embody wolf medicine is to awaken leadership that's fierce, tender, and true.

Only then will your leadership stop being performed and become prayer.

Wolf is waiting.
The pack is calling.
And your howl is needed.
All my love on your journey.

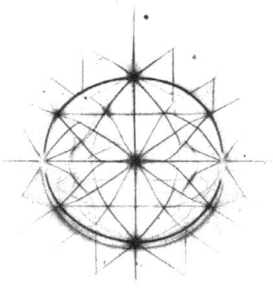

Chapter 1

THE SACRED DANCE

Honoring the Divine Masculine and Feminine Within
Angel Gold

𝕸y 𝕾t⊕ry

"Come to my house for two weeks and see what you think."

WTF. I just met this human. I have spent four days at a retreat with him previously, and now he wants me to go to a different country to visit for two whole weeks, during the lockdown? Am I crazy to say yes?

I started challenging myself when I asked myself if I was crazy by repeating the mantra given to me by one of my first shamanic mentors, "If you are sane enough to contemplate whether or not you are crazy, you aren't." Dropping in and listening to my body, the "yes" was authentic, and so began my next adventure, marked by my 50th birthday portal.

Two weeks turned into flowing with more "yes" as we did the sacred dance. I chose to lean into my omega feels, surrendering and allowing myself, for the first time in my life, to be consciously led by an alpha captain in the fire service.

The wiggles were real, forcing me to surrender to depths I had never swum in. His capacity to 'out-warrior' me was strong, which allowed my goddess to peek her head out and experiment with the mystery surrounding her while I felt safe and held in this space.

Soon into our courtship, an adventure called as the world attempted to navigate COVID and the restrictions put upon us humans. One warrior said "no" to the institution that was challenging his beliefs about vaccinations, and he made choices to leave his community and go where his values were accepted.

We said yes in support of this member of my alpha's pack and helped his family move from the West Coast all the way to the other side of the country via moving trucks.

The days turned to nights, and the sun came up and down as we drove across the country, state to state, entering different time zones, realities, and worlds. My consciousness expanded into the stars, sleeping, dreaming, driving, lulling me into lucidity as we covered 33 hours of road, stopping only to fuel and empty our truck and soul baskets.

Sleep came easily with the hum of the road, lulling me into dreamtime.

I was on my aunt and uncle's property in the mountains, visiting Uncle Jerry. Man, I haven't seen him in forever. His eyes were as sparkly as the last time I saw him. Was it yesterday? My heart was exploding with joy as we walked the property, through the trees, smelling the fresh mountain air. He talks about connection with the land through his eyes, with no words escaping his half-shaven face. Memories flash of our most heartfelt moments in this lifetime, reminding me how special this soul was to me in its human form.

Sunlight blinds me, searing into my eyelids, forcing my consciousness to wake into the here and now as the sun greets another day. As I sit up, feeling the vibration of the highway beneath my hip, I smile, thinking: *What a great visit with Uncle Jerry. Wait a minute, he's been dead for 20 years.*

My body freezes as I come to full consciousness, looking around my unique environment and processing where I just was. I glance down at my soul basket, reminding myself where I am, who I am with, and what we're doing. I softly run my hands down my arms, leaning into the cozy nest of furry blankets and sacred space created in the cab of the moving truck. A smile greets my face as I look out the window at the passing trees. "I am in my own mitote ceremony," I comment to myself, taking in the beauty of the rising sun.

We're helping this family to move across the country, honoring their decision not to vaccinate and relocate their eight children and two dogs to the East Coast. Members of the pack are starting a new life and storyline in a different part of the country. These are experiences that allow me to practice unconditional love and stand in my power, supporting humans where they are.

The ocean called, and this family answered. We are witnessing wolves stand in their power, honor their internal guidance, and follow their instinct to be of service in a different community. They are not backing down from those who question and attempt to subjugate the husband within his career. We are holding space for his wife as she births her eighth child during the last full moon, as they sell their family home and start packing for their new adventure, simultaneously welcoming a new baby girl into this world.

I am an outsider. Yet, I am in this truck, moving their life to South Carolina. Here, I have an opportunity to practice full goddess presence, resilience, and an open heart. There is an opportunity to stay expanded in the wife's presence of judgment and unacceptance, as I am 'the other woman.' I challenge her agreement that divorce is not okay in her Christian belief system.

I witness my body during the discomfort, acknowledging and supporting myself in solo practice. Thankful for the tools provided, I recite mantras, do breathwork, and honor my body by removing myself when my energy is too low to maintain my nervous system as she slowly works through her own agreements.

We acknowledge the death cycle she is in. New baby, new home, a new state, new life, as she wrangles eight children in the middle of a pandemic as her alpha chooses to leave his job. I repeat the mantra: new baby, new home, new state, new life as I practice not taking her distance personally.

I am overwhelmed by the chaos of the moving trucks being unloaded by the three firefighters who drove across the country to help their brother and his family, part of their pack.

The beach calls to me, the sand between my toes, songs sung by passing birds, the sun sinking into and activating my cells as the waves softly roll into shore, alignment. This is sacred ground; tears fill my eyes as I scan the beach, "I could live here." I hear myself speak aloud, heart expanding, anchoring a container of energy, knowing deep within that I will return another day or lifetime to this beach. Or have I just returned?

The vibrations of the truck become a welcome initiation deep within myself, allowing and leaning into the stream of consciousness, recapitulating and rewriting storylines where I gave my own power away, sending healing to those timelines and releasing myself from those stories holding me back. I am dreaming, awake, following time with the movement of the sun. What day is it?

I feel expansion unlike ever before, embodying the present moment, forgetting there was even a moving truck in the parking lot at the Opryland Resort in Nashville on our one night of reprieve, in the process of moving a family.

Did we escape the matrix? I ask as we walk down hallways with no people in them. Stores are closed; restaurants are dark with no movement. There's creepy silence, and I joke about the fog outside looking like 'zombie weather.' *Are they hiding in here? Where is everyone? Is this simulator just for us at this moment?*

The carpet in the halls mesmerizes us into a hypnotic state every time we leave our room. I touch the walls as we walk, gazing into the sparkly lights on the ceiling. *Is this place real?* A noise pulls my attention, "Oh look! There is a human," he sings with the voice of an angel.

The soft, downy bed is a welcome change from the bench of the truck. Stretching out, I allow my soul-basket freedom and movement as I snuggle into the comfort and darkness of this new space. I find myself drifting off into a previous vision; it is so dark outside.

With the vision of the Eagle, I witness:

This parking lot is expansive in the black of night. The huge building is blocking the wind as the family works to fix the bus-like RV parked against the brick building. There are tubes protruding from the bottom and sides. All are working tirelessly to fix the electrical system and restart the bus so they can carry on to their next destination.

One by one, the tubes are untangled and cut until only one remains. Jose slowly walks the perimeter of the bus and joins the family inside.

Time stands still as peace and reverence fill the air; stillness settles into space. The generations of the family quietly gather inside the bus, breathing in unison, merging with the infinite, as he is called home.

Waking up from my dream, moisture held in my eyes as my heart holds space for my loved ones. I turn on my computer and write. . .

Hearts
traversing in the infinite
Grazing past the stars and moon
Hearing calls from heaven
She called him home so soon

Honoring an
abandoned temple
Showering love
in a different tune
Grateful for this journey
Gratitude for you
Your love, your heart
your everything,
Inspires my heart's truth

Daring domestication
allowing our souls to thrive
We came to Earth

in avatars
Knowing the risk
to be alive

Our birthright
Our song
If the world could just get along
Peace and love
comes in all forms of size
I pray the world
one day
will come to realize

Blessings to you for lighting the way
shining your bright light
As you whisper
words of wisdom. . .
I hear you in the night.

The sun peeks into the room, into my eyes, gently bringing me back into the soft, downy bed. I am filled with love and gratitude for this journey and space, and the humans who have chosen to join me in this storyline. Stepping into the parking lot of the Opryland Resort, greeting the full moon in all its glory, I take a moment to honor don Miguel Ruiz's brother, who crossed over the night before.

Breathe.

I am ready for the next part of this magical adventure I am on.

Feral and free, the full moon and me
Feral and free
the full moon and me
Sparkly lights
Shining down
shedding light
on the now

Presence is truth
the light shines so bright
My love
My heart
Beams gratitude for this night

Sea salt drips from my wet hair as we find our seats on the plane. I'm settling in and allowing the expansion room to play, drifting in and out, recapitulating what comes into my awareness, as the plane lulls me into lucidity.

Hours drift by, the sun long into slumber, our last plane to catch missed by minutes in the dark of night. My warrior within perks up: The *boys are on a 48-hour shift at 8 a.m. It's midnight, and we're in Seattle. Three and a half hours from home with no flights left tonight. Okay. I am driving. Scanning the airport, where's Starbucks? I need coffee.*

Don't make assumptions, I hear from deep within.

I pass along my thought process to my partner, who instantly rejects the offer. "Nah, I'm fine."

"But you both must work tomorrow, and I don't. You unpacked the entire truck by yourself today, then went surfing, then got on a plane that crossed the entire country!"

"This is what we do. We are doers."

Witnessing my jaw clenching and the fire building in my belly, I got still and checked in with my body:

Hey, love, what's going on?

I am capable of leading.
I felt like I was not doing enough unloading the trucks
because I physically could not; this I can do.
I KNOW how tired they both are, driving that tired is a safety issue,
I will not sleep anyways
I have been expanded in goddess energy the whole trip;
my warrior is not being acknowledged at this moment.
Oh, he is forgetting we made an agreement to be agile with our aspects.
I need to use different language.
Thank you.

I turn to my partner and look deep into his eyes, "Hey Alpha, this is a perfect opportunity for you to practice being willing to receive."

An hour goes by as he stands alone in line getting the rental. As we head to the car, I inform the young cub I will be driving. The same dialogue shows up; the banter and giggles commence around their fast lifestyle and lack of sleep being normal in their world. This time, I just smiled and sent him so much love, knowing seeds will be planted tonight. I practice patience with the wolf cubs.

The little one chooses to drive first. He pops in the front seat, and I slide in the passenger seat, while my partner lies across the back with my furry blanket. At 1 a.m. I poke him, "Are you ready to switch?" He chooses the destination where we will switch, crawls into the back seat, and accepts the furry blanket offering.

An hour into my drive, the warrior beside me wakes, checks the GPS, and starts to talk. Interrupting him, "Aren't you supposed to be sleeping?" I grin, running my hand along the inside of his leg and up to his chest, settling on his heart, "I got you." I energetically beam into his weary eyes, witnessing his body surrender and slide into a deep sleep.

I pulled into the driveway of the house left behind to drop off the warrior cub at his truck. Stirring, he exclaims, "Did you drive the rest of the way home? You brought me to my truck? Awesome!"

"I got you," escapes my lips, as he gathers his belongings and waves to my partner as he climbs into his vehicle. "See you in a couple of hours, Captain."

The alarm clock goes off after two hours of restful sleep in our own bed. "Thank you for taking care of me." He whispers as he kisses my third eye and leaves to be in service to the citizens of our community, once again with his pack.

The start of a new day.

The Medicine

Routines kill creativity. Yet, humans also need routines.

Where is the balance?

When your routine is so hardwired, you slip into autopilot and miss a lot of what is going on around you. Your light, awareness, and sensitivities shut down.

The art of awareness demands creativity, attention, and intention.

Can you undo some of your conscious patterning?

Or rather, are you *ready* to undo some of your conscious patterning?

You are wildly capable, and you always have a choice.

Start with something little, like brushing your teeth with the opposite hand or taking a different route to get to work. How about ordering something different off the menu, or choosing a different type of music to listen to?

My big undoing experiment was to not drive when I came to Washington.

As a powerful, independent, single woman for years, being in control of my life was my normal. I chose to allow my partner to always be the one to drive, to be the consciousness, to be alpha, and lead. I chose not to memorize the roads and just be in the moment when we were in the vehicles, and completely surrender to the experience.

I had to train my body to sit with the discomfort of not being in control. I had to train my brain not to try to remember the roads or where anything was and just be in the moment.

This was a big ask for me, as a recovering controller. Control your environment, control your safety. Right? Does anyone else get nervous when someone else is driving?

I chose to stay in the experiment until I became comfortable with just being in the vehicle. Then, I started mapping the area and driving myself again.

Where can you be more present in your life and **shed some light** onto some unhealthy patterns that are holding you back?

Six steps to release the snare around your paw:

1. Meet yourself where you are at.
2. Do not set yourself up for failure.
3. Choose attainable goals.
4. Assess and repeat.
5. Have fun with it!
6. Share your experience in the group.

Remember, the art of awareness demands creativity, attention, and intention.

Sharing your intention allows the Universe an opportunity to support you and your soul's growth in many magical and mysterious ways, yay!

Mama Willow is so proud

of her wolf cubs and loves to post their works of art on our den walls.

You deserve to be seen, you gorgeous ray of light!

You can find my contact information at the back, in the "About the Author" page.

ENERGETIC AGILITY IS THE SECRET SAUCE TO KEEP
AUTHENTICITY ALIVE IN MODERNIZED GENDER ROLES.

~ANGEL GOLD

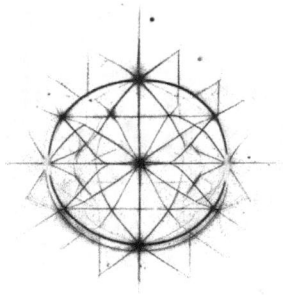

Chapter 2

YOUR LIGHT IS YOUR STRENGTH

Children of the Sun Embody Leadership, Beginning and Ending With Love

Jorge Luis Delgado

My Story

In the Andean tradition, we learn the most important messages from legends and stories that our grandfathers told us about the different experiences of life.

Examples that inspire us humans to take initiative.
How we can arrive at diverse levels of awareness.

One of these beautiful legends tells the story of a searcher who was successful in many aspects of life. He was successful in his career, had a nice family, a good car, and a house. It seemed that he was successful, but he knew something was missing. He was empty inside, so he decided to explore what would complete him and how he could experience his real self on a different level.

Success only in the material world is not all we're searching for.

He tried many ways and many modalities to try to fill that emptiness. He looked at politics, religions, and many kinds of movements and groups of people.

Suddenly, he got some news about people living in the mountains with a unique way of life. They are very connected with Mother Earth and the Father Sun.

Every experience is good, and part of our life learning, and everything we learn is preparing us to be the leaders of the new cycle.

He got all that experience and went to this community in the highlands. He found that there were many elders and wise people up there, so he decided to look for the oldest one. He thought that the oldest elder should have the deepest level of consciousness about awareness and how to find the real self.

When he arrived at this elder's house, he asked, "Grandfather, could you tell me what it is you can teach me?"

He said, "Yes. What is it that you want to learn?"

"I want to learn about my love." He had to start at some point, and he thought that after all his experiences, it was all about love.

The elder says, "Well, if you want to expand your love, the only thing you must do is share your love. No matter what, just share your love."

The searcher responds, "This is too simple. Maybe you can teach me a little bit deeper. I have the time and the money because I'm taking all this year for myself. I want to go deeper than this."

The elder says, "You know, it's quite simple. You must experience sharing your love with all your relations. With your mother, father, family, neighbors, your past, your future, and yourself."

"Okay. Then I can do it by myself?"

"Yes. You must do it by yourself. Nobody else is going to do it for you.

Only you can do that."

When he returned home, he was extremely helpful to everybody. The family, the neighbors, and everybody who needed help. He would be the first one there.

He felt good assisting and helping people, but at some point, he still felt that emptiness. He decided to return to the community in the highlands to talk to the elder.

He said, "Grandfather, could you tell me what I'm doing wrong here? I can really feel that feeling of good actions, but I'm still feeling that emptiness inside. What am I doing wrong?"

The elder said, "Okay. Let's see. How much more do you love yourself since the last time you were here?"

"Wait a moment. You never told me to love myself. You said to share your love with others."

"Yes, but if you do not know the frequency of that energy. If you do not experience love for yourself, how do you know what you're sharing is love? How do you know what you're sharing is light? Remember that light is always wise, like love is always in service."

"Oh. That is a key point. I must learn how to love myself deeper." "Yes. You got it."

He returned home and was learning deeper modalities to love himself. He found that being in gratitude is a way of love. To be grateful for all parts of his body, with life, and the relations. Everything was amazing for him just by being grateful.

His mind was watching and saying, *You got it. You are in a higher level of consciousness of love.*

He was excited and went to the elder again to confirm that he was already on the higher level of consciousness of love. Love is 'munay', and 'tucuy munay niyoc' is a higher level of consciousness of love. When he was asking if he was already at tucuy munay niyoc, the elder immediately said, "You are not there yet, my friend."

He was disappointed and returned home. After a while, he explored all the ways to love himself because he wanted to get to this higher level of consciousness of love. He experienced much coming from the heart, but one of the most amazing experiences was loving children. To love the inner child.

He thought that was it. When he arrived at the elder again, he asked, "Am I at tucuy munay niyoc?"

"You are not there yet."

He then learned a way to use warm words with himself. Positive words and thoughts. He went back to the elder and said, "Now I can warmly talk with myself, with much affection. Soft, and I always talk the truth to myself, because I can speak from my heart."

"You are doing very well, but you are not there yet."

"Really?!"

"Yes."

He returned home, trying to find other ways.

This time, when he returned to the home of the elder, the elder could see him coming from a distance and called out to him, "Hey, my friend. You are not there yet."

"What? What do you mean? I did not even tell you what kind of experiences I've been having."

"Well, all that is not important, because it's just your mind. You're just in the mind that wants approval. Your mind wants a certificate that you're doing it and are in the higher level of love."

The truth is, it's the cosmos that tells you you are there.

You just feel it.

You just open all the doors, and you understand all this as part of the experience. Then the cosmos sends you a messenger. In this case, it's a hummingbird that flies above your head trying to get the nectar from you, because you opened the resistance naturally without the mind.

When all your discernment is in your heart, then you're open to sharing your sweetness, affection, nectar, beauty, light, and life.

That means you understand life as one, you are wise, and you are love, but you must try it first, as the hummingbird does, without destroying the flower. Each of us, as we grow, needs to have strong roots with Mother Earth and a strong connection with Father Sun, so we can bloom any place, anywhere.

I wish you many hummingbirds in your life.

In this new day in this new world, it's so important to know everyone is in an evolutionary process.

In this process, we can see clearly that the process has to do with all our relations. In whatever we do in this lifetime, we impact our surroundings internally and externally. We are all interconnected; we are all interdependent as we are one community of children of the light. We have this great opportunity to bring our strength from our inner sun, from our real self, to bring the evolution for the expansion of consciousness.

In my beloved country of Peru, recently, people have been arguing about the idea of having a new constitution for our country. Some people believe that the transformation will happen through love. Some people believe a new constitution will bring happiness, freedom, or joy. But within each of us, we know that only in the pathway of the evolution of our consciousness lies the opening of the endless spring of love; service and wisdom from our hearts is the only way.

But as much awareness we bring about the meaning of that light, we can see that the leaders of the evolving world must be leaders who love themselves. There are no new leaders who do not love themselves. Because if you do not love yourself, you do not love Mother Earth, and you do not love your relations. It's important to accept your inner wisdom.

Listening to our hearts harmonizes our relations.

Everybody will make an important contribution to the evolution of life.

Releasing resistance, releasing the blockages that do not let us be who we are, is our first mission. We have the ability; we have the gifts to transform. We use the qualities of the light that Father Sun is teaching us every day: clarifying our past, creating transparency in our lives, and accepting the luminosity of our luminous bodies. Accepting the gifts and talents we bring, we can share the brightness of our souls and the brightness of our hearts. Of course, together with our bright minds.

New leadership starts by loving ourselves.

The new leadership continues by sharing that love.

Sharing our love makes us and our gifts stronger and stronger. Diving into the mysteries of life, surrendering, and discovering new rays of light in this new world will give you opportunities to grow, expand, and find new gifts you didn't know you had. Perhaps you don't know exactly what the biggest gift is that we receive from Mother Earth, life, the cosmos, and our relations. For sure, we will realize the most important gift we can give to ourselves is to feed our souls and nurture them to let the light of the mother and the father come through our experiences of life.

Many of us on this planet and across the world have been planting seeds of knowledge for this new society, dreaming of the new world, and planning to build new communities connected in light. All the seeds exist for humanity; it's now possible for all of humanity to bloom. Within this blooming, there is also a deep need for rooting in. It's essential to have deep roots to make our relationship stronger with Mother Earth.

Mother Earth is calling for humanity to help open the resistance to the light. Open to the love, service, and wisdom of Father Sun.

Every day Father Sun shares with us. As much as we consciously choose to connect with that light, we embody that light, and we become more aware that light is love. We are aware that no light is not wise.

The light is always wise, so we always choose light.

We always know that light is in service to the light. The new evolutionary success in leadership focuses on our natural, authentic ability to bring our contribution to life on this planet. In this life, everything is reciprocal. Reciprocity happens in our lives from different directions; it's multi-dimensional. And it's happening right now as we connect with this valuable tool. Heart-centered awareness, living from your intuition, and being in a consistent space of being in service will reflect that unique ray of light to you in your own life.

We have the most important strength, our power, which is light.

For our ancestors, the Incas, light is power—the power that stays forever. Anchoring the new light for the new world is building foundations for the new society and the new paradigms that have to do with the most important meaning of life, the new Pachacuti.

The return to the sun, the return to light,
the return to sacredness, the return to the divine.

It's from the divine self that we can harmonize ourselves and our duality. We can harmonize life. It starts with the love that we open to ourselves.

The society of love is the society of wisdom reflected in the way we experience life, and naturally, we are harmonizing all our relations.

The Medicine

To feed and nourish our souls and allow ourselves to bloom, we must connect to the sun and embody its light. Ceremonies and practices may support your evolution by helping you step into your birthright as a Child of the Sun.

Before doing any ceremony, it's important to review and set your intent. This is especially true when we're releasing the debilitating energy of Hucha (dark energies).

Intent plays with the world of possibilities, and with the Divine Mother, everything is possible.

No matter what has happened or how much we're suffering, the intent in our hearts will always be connected to the Universe. It's vital for us to enter into these powerful, healing ceremonies with a pure, clear purpose. We must demonstrate our conviction and commitment to self-healing by doing these ceremonies wholeheartedly.

The most important thing is to go into the ceremony with an open heart and participate using the purest part of yourself, and request permission from Mother Earth and the spirits that reside in that sacred space.

Understanding the differences between intent and intention is also important during the ceremony. Intent comes from your heart and is connected to your life force energy, from which all your visions and possibilities are born. Intention comes from your brain and is based on expectations and rationalizations.

To release the Hucha within takes the heart life force of your intent.

GREETINGS OF THE SUN PRACTICE

We, as descendants of the Inka, have many ways of liberating ourselves from Hucha and overcoming heavy energies. In this greeting of the sun practice, we gain energy as we surrender our darkness over to the light and connect our own cosmic energy to Father Sun and Mother Earth in an encounter of high intensity.

1. Find a place where you can see Father Sun in the east. Lift your head to the sun and invite the light into your cells with your arms outstretched as you breathe deep within your lungs. Eyes can be open or closed as you show gratitude for this moment.

2. Allow your arms to fall to your side as you allow yourself to merge with the rays of light. Reach to the light with your right hand and either in your head or aloud say the words "in love" as you grasp the filaments of the light in your hand and bring them to your heart and hold the nourishing energy in your chest.

3. With your left hand, reach to the light and either in your head or aloud, say the words "without fear" as you grasp the filaments of the light in your hand and bring them to your sacral area, holding the light to transmute any dark energies residing within. As you feel it bubble up, pull it out with your left hand, away from your

body, and direct it toward Mother Earth to transmute into pure light.

4. Repeat as many times as needed to feel your clear channel open and flowing. Allow yourself to be nourished by this light, and as it starts to overflow, extend that love to humanity. The power, from where we share the love we have within, comes from this clear place.

5. The deeper you surrender, the more you experience the light. Keep your intent in the forefront of your heart as you connect your own inner sun to the light of Father Sun.

1. Connection to the sun is key not only to the energy but also to the humans, plants, and animals surrounding you. Look to a person, plant, or animal and share your light with them as they reflect you, your unique ray of light, and allow that energy to flow through you.

2. You will remember, in this heightened state of awareness, you are one with all there is.

Gratitude, love, service, and wisdom are medicine.

Jorge Luis Delgado was born in the Andes mountains of Peru.

He is a descendant of Quechua and Aymara native cultures. A lover of ancient wisdom, Jorge Luis became a "chakaruna" (bridge person) at the age of 11 and began to assist and show Pilgrims and travelers how to find their way.

He shares his solar heritage all over the world, including North, Central, and South America, Europe, and Asia. As a founding member of the Brotherhood of the Solar Disk society, he is a way-shower for this 10th Pachakuti in this world that is now being turned upside down.

He is known and respected by the Andean Priests, Priestesses, and the Indigenous people of the region and has been highlighted on the TV show *Ancient Aliens* in over ten episodes.

As a great organizer of world events and an activator of portals and the expansion of consciousness, Jorge teaches that a new consciousness is emerging, one leading to a golden age that was activated in 2012.

He is the owner and founder of Kontiki Tour Company and owns hotels in Cusco, the sacred valley, Aguas Calientes (Machu Picchu), and on the shores of Lake Titicaca.

He is a keeper of ancient knowledge and uses it to assist in healing for all who are ready.

To go on one of his sacred power journeys or to connect further with Jorge, see below.

Connect with Jorge:

Website: https://www.kontikiperu.com

Email: Kontiki@kontikiperu.com

Facebook: https://www.facebook.com/jorgeluis.delgado.311/

Instagram: https://www.instagram.com/jorgeluischakaruna

WE HAVE THE MOST IMPORTANT STRENGTH, OUR POWER, WHICH IS LIGHT. THE LIGHT IS ALWAYS WISE, SO WE ALWAYS CHOOSE LIGHT."

~JORGE LUIS DELGADO

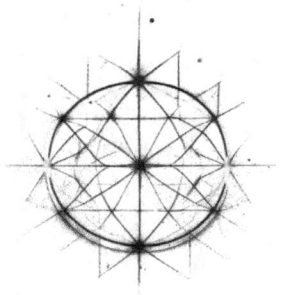

Chapter 3

MEDICINE WALK

A Path of Direct Revelation

Atlantis Wolf

Why bother connecting to spiritual realms? You could save your life. I saved mine.

Shamanism is ritualized animism, the ancient belief that everything we can see and touch is animated with a soul, a spiritual component married to a physical form. A shaman practices connecting to that unseen terrain, normally with their eyes covered or closed, using ceremonies aligned with the spirals of planetary cycles and human rites of passage. The word shaman means 'one who sees in the dark.'

Shamanism is a spiritual practice based on direct revelation. You are your own shaman. There is no guru, priest, or rabbi leading the way. Your personal experience in shamanic journeys and rituals gives you the answers you need if you are practicing with integrity. Detach your ego from the outcome and ask spirit guides for help. Ask from a place of love, not fear. Spirit guides do not have physical bodies. They might come to you in your mind's eye in the form of animals, ancestors, or angels. Or even dragons.

My Story

"Bruce, I'm running off to work!" I shouted up the stairs from the kitchen as I pulled on my second boot and snapped my purple coat off its hook.

"Okay, Mom, see you soon," he replied from behind his closed bedroom door.

One of my black cats, Pontos, sat his meatball-sized body next to his empty food bowl and turned his bear cub cheeks and green eyes at me as I shoved my cell phone into my purse, slung my bag with massage sheets over my shoulder, and grabbed my lunch from the fridge.

Dammit, I thought.

"Bruce, can you feed the cats their tuna fish?" I shouted. "And scoop the litter? I don't have time."

"Yep," he answered.

I hurried to the garage, snatching the mail from the mailbox. As I walked and shuffled through the mail, I saw a letter with the return address of the City of Amherst, New York.

Dammit to hell, I thought as I dumped it and my bags on the passenger seat and started my car.

I forgot to call in for the speeding ticket I got over the holiday break in Buffalo. First one in years. Years! I missed my chance to get the fine reduced.

I called my friend, John, whom I always call on my way to work. "Hiya!" I said.

"Good morning!" he replied, "How are you, Sunshine?"

"Pretty good, rushing off to work. I'm free this Thursday if you want to go out to dinner at L'Albatros or somewhere close."

He said, smiling, "I feel like you're always rushing to work. Thursday is great. Let's talk on Wednesday. I have to take this call."

I drove past my favorite nature reserve and saw a hawk perched on a high branch.

It must be nice to be just sitting there, I thought. *No time to ask for a message today, my friend. I'm running late, maybe on my way home.*

I careened through the familiar bends and curves past the green parklands and blue lake into my last right turn. One residential city block away from work. Last lap in the home stretch.

Ha! I thought. *I'm totally going to make it. I've got four minutes!*

I slowed to a pause as I came up to my stop sign, looking right at Roxboro school's soccer field, bounded by the long stretch of chain link fence. I swiveled my head left—empty street. Back to the right quick as a bird. Oversized white Ford pickup truck to my right, pulling into the driveway of the stone century house on the corner.

Yes! I thought. *All good.*

I accelerated, zipping over the cross-street. Halfway across in the middle of the road, a curved flash of tan appeared to my right, outside my passenger door. It was so close I couldn't even see the bumper. But I saw the logo on the hood—Nissan.

Oh no! I thought, sucking in all my breath. Time switched to slo-mo video mode.

The black bumper crashed into my red Volkswagen at the crossbar between the front and back doors, shattering the glass windows. The impact on the metal body came with a sound of an elephant's groan and a rippling wave of energy that tossed my head and neck first to the right, then left, into my driver's side window with a stone-like crack. The front passenger tire was pushed inward, straining at the axle, as the back end of the car was beginning to spiral into oncoming traffic.

The moment unfolded around me as if I were sitting at the center of a white thousand-petal lotus, opening petal by petal. I thought,

Double-dammit! I'll have to get the car fixed. If it can be fixed. Am I hurt? Feel fine. Kinda wavy. What if I have to stop working again? Rent. Mortgage. I'll have to tell my dad. I'll be late for work. I don't have time for this. Oh! This might be bad. Super bad. My head is going to hit the window again. That's going to hurt. This might be worse than I can imagine. Lights out? The end?

I closed my eyes, letting go of the choking tension circling around my body like a claw, and whispered, "No."

Darkness swallowed me. A moment of black silence, nothingness.

Stillness.

I arrived in the driver's seat of my car, parked in front of the stone house on the corner. My body was uninjured, and my car was undamaged. I looked around. *All good,* I thought. I looked through my window to the left and saw the tan Nissan sedan. He had stopped, back brake lights on. He saw me looking at him and then drove away.

What happened? I thought. I felt my body as if I had long antennae that were checking all of my skin. *All good.* My heartbeat was even and calm. There was no adrenaline pumping into my bloodstream. I couldn't have been steadier. My brain and body felt slow, like waking from a long afternoon nap in an empty house.

The car phased through your car, I heard my angel voice say in my head.

Oh, okay, I thought. *Sure. Like that story Grace told about her Chicago business trip. Okay. Okay. I'm okay. Okay, I'm going to work now. Do I work?*

I eased my foot off the brake and began to drive down the long, tree-lined block with turn-of-the-century duplexes and three-story apartment buildings. It was sunny with a few clouds—a cool late-winter morning.

I heard two voices in my head, a child and an adult.

The adult's voice was saying things like: *How could that happen? Maybe it didn't happen. You could have been killed! You should be ashamed of yourself for not seeing that car. You're lucky to be alive. Don't tell anybody! What would Bruce think? Or your dad? He's paying for that car, you know.*

The child's voice was saying things like: *Wow! That was amazing! That might be the coolest thing that has ever happened to me in my life. Man! Can't wait to tell Karla. This is out there even for me! I love how the sun comes through those tree branches. It'll be nice when the leaves come back. I'm so lucky this is my commute. I love seeing this neighborhood every day. Oh, now that's a pretty dog. What a floofy tail!*

I found a parking spot close to the back door and came to a stop. Two minutes early.

Amazing! I thought.

As I walked up the stairs, the adult voice grew louder. *You're late. It's not professional. The client will be angry.* I stumbled at the last step, slowing down to open the landing door. My client was waiting on a chair in the hallway.

"Hi, Fred!" I said. "Sorry, I'm late."

Fred looked at his watch and said, "Looks like you're right on time."

We walked into my office, and I turned on the Turkish lamp and pedestal knight lamp in the reception room, then the salt lamp and fairy lights in the center room. I set my bags in my Zoom room before heading to the massage room.

"Your room is ready," I said to him. "You can head in. I'll give you a second and knock before I come in."

He walked into the massage room, closing the door behind him. I walked back into my Zoom room, hung up my coat and purse, and took off my boots, slipping into my red wool slippers with a felt black cat design across the top.

I picked up my black hematite dragon figure and closed my eyes, holding it against my chest. In my mind's eye, my black guardian dragon with blue kyanite eyes appeared, surrounding me with his massive, warm, scaly body.

What was all that? I asked him.

Schism, he answered.

Oh, I replied. I'm okay? You made a choice, he said.

I inhaled a short breath and exhaled an elongated sigh, grinning at my galactic dragon and his wide smile filled with 10,000 teeth. I opened my eyes and placed the figure back on the shelf.

I walked toward the massage room door. I knocked, turning the doorknob.

"All good?" I asked with a smile as I stepped inside.

ΨHE ΜEDICINE

The longer version of my story is that I was getting intuitive messages about getting into a car accident for months. I ignored them. I thought it was residual, ancestral energy I was healing. My grandmother was in a car accident in her 20s and never drove again. Both ideas could be true.

I believe my moment of clarity, my choice point, was possible because of my connection to Spirit—also because of my autism. My whirling brain is quick to analyze and assess. My connection to the spiritual world is a constant practice, as automatic as breathing. I shift between the physical and non-physical world every day as part of my work with massage and coaching clients. It's part of my human experience. I think of myself as a ferryman, taking people into the mist and back again. I share what I see and hear, then teach my clients how to do it.

My baseline practice is waking up and walking from my house into the woods. Everyday. In all weather (except sleet). Connecting to nature helps me feel part of the natural world, not separated from it. Forest bathing helps me find my pace when I'm unchained from deadlines, schedules, or knowing the day of the week.

I live in a historic city suburb on Lake Erie. Developed in the 1920s, it has three lakes surrounded by forest. If you look in your community, you may be surprised to find a patch of forest or natural environs close to your home, too. Find somewhere you can be surrounded by trees, water, or rock formations.

'Medicine walk' is the phrase used by the shamanic community to mean a walking ceremony or to walk with the intention of asking Mother Nature a question. You can think of it as opening yourself to guidance while immersing yourself in a natural setting. There is no set amount of time required. Take as long as you need. I usually walk for 60 to 90 minutes.

You can follow my guidelines or come with me on a walk in this YouTube video. https://youtu.be/1TMbD0coJsQ

ACCOMMODATIONS:

You might be thinking: *But, Atlantis, I can't walk for an hour. I can't even walk for five minutes! I don't live close to a forest or ocean. I'm too busy. I'm too old. I'm scared. It won't work for me.*

Start where you are. Set your own pace. Make accommodations for yourself. Meet yourself where you are today. Go out your front door and walk for a few minutes, then turn around and walk back. Walk four minutes today and five minutes tomorrow. A single tree works as well as a forest. A brook can guide you as well as an ocean. Your body will respond each time you practice, even if you are only walking in your imagination.

WHAT TO BRING:

1. Layers of clothing to be comfortable as you get your inner fire going.

2. Small water bottle.

3. Dried fruit in case you walk longer than you intended and need a light snack.

4. Comfortable, closed-toed shoes. Walk with authority and keep your toes safe for walking on stones, dirt, mud, and puddles.

WHAT NOT TO BRING:

1. A cell phone. We are socially conditioned to be available 24/7. For some people, it's a habit; for others, an addiction. Unplug—phone off, heart open. If you need help, your spirit guides will

send someone with a phone to help. You don't need it. You're just conditioned to have it. Free yourself for one hour a day.

2. Anything related to a cell phone, such as an Apple watch, Fitbit, or heart rate monitor. If it beeps or burps, leave it at home.

3. A dog. This is not about multitasking. This is the time for you to open yourself to inner wisdom. Walk your wolf before or after.

4. A buddy. This is a solo adventure, a spiritual practice. This hour is for you to discover your own interior landscape reflected in the outer world. This is not about your partner pointing things out for you. It's all about you, Love.

INTENTION SETTING

A ceremony is setting an intention and performing an intuitive ritual. Set your intention and choose your ritual. For example, I like to set the intention, 'Show me what I need to see today.' As a ritual, I like to hang my walking clothes over the towel rack in the bathroom the night before, so I can put them on without a thought. I like to put my socks in my shoes downstairs for the same reason. In the morning, I squeeze a lemon wedge into a glass and add water to start my daily digestion. I save coffee as my cup of celebration when I return from my triumphant walk. Another success!

SAMPLE INTENTIONS

- Observe your breath and how it changes over the walk.
- Look at patterns in tree trunks.
- How many animals do you see?
- Listen to your heartbeat.

SAMPLE RITUALS

- Set out your favorite fruit and cut it silently when you return, easing back into home life. Imagine where it came from, how it grew, and how it got to you.

- Step outside and breathe three times, in through your nose and out through your mouth as long as you can on the exhale. Then begin walking.

- Before you walk back into your house, greet your house with love and gratitude. Say, "Thank you for being my house (or apartment or room)."

- Make coffee or tea in silence, thanking everyone who had to work to provide you with the cup of coffee or tea in your hand.

THE WALK

As you walk, become the observer. Move from thinking to feeling, from your mind into your body. Give yourself permission to treat what is happening as a movie. Watch the movie. Begin to notice how each of your senses is reacting.

- Do you see birds, trash on the sidewalk, or details in the houses close to you?

- Do you feel the wind on your skin, the sun, or the humid air?

- How do your feet feel as they walk? Do you walk heel-to-toe or midfoot-to-toe? Does one leg feel longer than the other? Do you walk fast, slow, or somewhere in between? How do your hips feel?

Keep walking. Keep noticing. What is hooking your attention? What do you see or feel today? Do you see animal footprints or scat? Do you see birds in the sky? Do you notice which trees hold a bigger space than others?

AFTER THE WALK

Resist the urge to grab your phone. Breathe in your home space. Notice how it feels today. Observe the way the light fills your kitchen. Come back to your home routines with grace and a slowed pace. Remember what you observed in your walk and write it in a journal. Sit with your coffee or tea and journal into each of your senses, including emotions. Commit to journaling for ten minutes each day immediately after your walk. Then once a week, go back and read what you wrote.

As an experiment, write one word that describes your mood before you walk and one word after. Then play with other ideas, like focusing on one sense each day or looking at how sunlight illuminates things on the ground versus things in bushes or trees. Notice the clouds. Listen to the wind. There is no limit to what you can notice. You can look at my Instagram page to see what I notice on my medicine walks. It's the same walk every day, but there is always something new to notice. It's a new day. And you are new to each other.

As you continue to practice your medicine walk, you see the world as a reflection of yourself. It's always okay to feel your feelings. But try to walk those feelings into a natural setting and set your intention to breathe into them. Allow them to move through you and inform you. What is triggering you? What is the root cause or original wound creating the vibration of anger in your body?

You have the answers to your questions. You know your wounds, have the diagnosis to treat your disease, and are your own healer. Walk with your questions. Breathe into your emotions. Observe your surroundings and open yourself to how they reflect your mind. What reality are you projecting? What dream are you creating with your words? It's all inside you. The journey within yourself is inevitable. Start now. Walk there. If you want help, I'm here—until I'm not.

I'm Atlantis Wolf, and I believe in you.

Atlantis Wolf is a Master Shamanic Breathwork facilitator and guide who helps people take the next step after they've had an unusual, mystical, or spiritual experience. She thinks of it as stepping into your labyrinth and walking back out with you.

As a licensed medical massage therapist, shamanic life coach, and emotional release therapist, she works with people in chronic pain. Her joy is connecting people to their spiritual counterparts using guided drumming meditations, Shamanic Breathwork ceremonies, and fire circles.

She was spiritually asleep until her mother's death awakened her gifts to communicate with spiritual beings, power animals, and galactic dragons. She remembers her past lives as an Egyptian healer, Toltec curandera, and Ayurvedic traveling shaman. She believes everyone has the capacity to be guided into their own transformational healing journey.

Atlantis grew up on a single-lane dirt road in rural Ohio, walking in the woods, whistling to birds, and asking: *Why am I here on Earth? What is calling me today?* She continues to walk to the trees at sunrise almost every day (except if it's sleeting) to listen to nature's reply.

She holds dual degrees in Civil Engineering and English and has worked as an environmental engineer, technical writer, franchise store owner, business analyst, project manager, licensed massage therapist, certified Emotion Code practitioner, marketing consultant, and entrepreneur.

Atlantis is a certified Master Shamanic Breathwork facilitator and ordained Shamanic Minister by Linda Star Wolf, Founder of Venus Rising Association for Transformation, and Seneca Wolf Clan lineage keeper. She is a certified Reiki Master by William Lee Rand, founder of the International Center for Reiki Training.

Atlantis is available for retreats, podcast interviews, and her favorite ceremony - Shamanic Breathwork and Cacao & Ecstatic Dance.

Connect with Atlantis:

Website: https://www.AtlantisWolf.com

Email: DragonMedicineWoman@gmail.com

YouTube: Atlantis Wolf

Instagram: https://www.instagram.com/dragonmedicinewoman

YOU CAN'T CHOOSE YOUR MOMENT OF CLARITY.

~M.E. ZONDRA

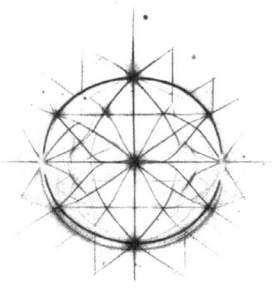

Chapter 4

FORCE OF NATURE

Burst Open Your True Energy

Eliza James

ᴍ̆y Sᴛᴏʀy

I am a boxer, baby!

I lace up my boxing shoes.

My feet are lit, and so is my path.

It is fucking early. I'm awakened from a deep sleep by an alarm. BAM!

It's time to break out of the dream world, where I do my best work, and bring these gifts into the physical world.

I am ready. I was born for this.

I find my way through the dark to turn on the lights. I pour myself a cup of hot coffee and sit in the stillness of the morning. I'm instantly filled with a deep sense of gratitude and great purpose. My early rising to the day supports my dedication and devotion to the life I've been gifted to lead and influence.

In here lives this depth of knowing; this is the one shot I've got. This is my first and last day. I visualize how I'll touch life today. My stomach turns with aliveness and excitement for the thrill of this energy exchange. My constant companion is my question:

What matters most, and how will I make that into physical matter?

My life force starts to break up the darkness of the night while shining light on the morning. My eyes start to twinkle with the stars from the cosmos; I can see more. My smile becomes bigger. My awakened dreams come to life. My heart opens and starts to pound with the eight billion beating hearts of Mother Earth.

I am alive and enlightened.

It is time to take it to the streets; this is the workout of my life.

There is much work to do.

My medium is boxing.

As I turn the knob to open the closed door, I grab the most integral instrument, my magical tool belt. Its contents assist me in the measurement of what I value most. To the untrained eye, this is just a bag of rocks. It's a container of magical crystals from the Earth and powerful invisible energy I've blended from information on the coordinates of space and time. I use this wise energy of the unconscious with the intent of bringing it to consciousness.

I pair this with the intelligent energy of the heart's consciousness.

The universal most powerful force.

The frequency of the universal mother is nurturing and protective.

I raise my vibrations; joy and enthusiasm are my fuel. Now full, I clip this on my waist. I open the door; roadwork is the first part of my practice as a boxer.

One foot in front of the other, I'm on my way to the boxing studio.

It's an eight-mile round trip to the boxing studio. Willing to go to any lengths, I go the distance. As I run through the quiet neighborhoods, I pass by all the people sleeping and wonder: *Am I the only one awake?*

The moon pours down her wisdom, and her reflection now guides my path. My stride picks up, and it's rhythmic with her waxing and waning, connecting my intuition. I drop deeper into my body and the depth of feeling offered here. I want to bring this feeling with me to my work. I have the eye of the tiger and the heart of the lion. I know that true strength comes from vulnerability and that I'm also a human being.

I will be brave enough to get to the heart of the matter.

My 10,000 hours turn into a mission.

My warm heart and the fire in my soul assist me on the cold winter morning.

Finally, I arrive at the boxing studio where I'm always greeted by a street cat named Scrappy. The whole place is illuminated by the cross I put on the building. There's a door; I have the key; I open it. The boxing bags are swaying, and the walls are painted. There's a powerful energy in this space.

Before I train anyone, I must train myself. I turn the music on and pull out some boxing wraps. There's a great sense of pride in wrapping my own hands for support with the wraps I created as the first female in history with a boxing brand.

I step over to the mirror to begin the next part of my practice, shadowboxing.

Shadowboxing is where a boxer practices their discipline in front of a mirror, like a dancer. I'm a southpaw, but I know how important it is to practice on both sides to meet somewhere in the middle. I get in an athletic stance, keep my elbows in, tight fists, and cover my face. The music is playing in the background; I start to dance and stay light on my feet. My feet are planted, rooted in the fiery core of the earth. I'm grounded.

Jab.

Right hand.

Straight down the middle. Back to my face.

Power and speed.

I catch my reflection in the mirror to check my form and start to question myself. My voice in my head becomes louder and drowns out the music. I start shadowboxing for real. In my reflection in the mirror, I see my dad's face.

His pain of losing his dad at three years old shows up. His heartbreak and worry as he took eight of his own kids at 28 years old and relocated as a single dad with a broken heart.

Jab! Jab! Jab!

His hard work ethic and great commitment to spiritual matters.

Jab! Jab! Jab!

His fear of death, his quiet power, he was frightening. His inability to manage his own emotions and always telling me not to be so sensitive and emotional. His great laugh. I sacrificed my life for him as a little girl. His brilliant, innovative ideas; he was a visionary. I have so much in common with his pain and his gifts.

I start to bounce.

I want to make him proud, and I do not want to be like him at all.

I reset.

Keep practicing, Eliza. Keep practicing.

A good song comes on. I see myself in the mirror.

I am sexy. I am strong. I am a boxer.

Jab cross. Jab cross. Jab cross.

The music gets quieter. I hear myself.

Who are you? So, you are a boxer? What does this mean to you? I have to be somebody in this world to matter. Think outside the box. What really matters,

Eliza? And what are you going to make into matter with your energy?

As a child, I always heard, "If I could bottle that energy you have, I would sell it."

Now you have bottled it. You are a boxer.

A champion.

What do you want to champion?

Keep breathing; stay in your base.

What will you do with this power and strength, Eliza?

Do you really want to train yourself to power over people and knock their lights out?

I thought you were about turning the lights on in people.

How are you going to be a champion?

How are you not going to continue all the physical abuse and violence you experienced?

The brass knuckles you bore on your cheek now add a dimple to your smile.

Your nose has been broken so many times, it's even now.

Are you going to pick competition over love?

Keep working it out, Eliza. Keep working.

You must become stronger to influence non-violence in the traditional sport of boxing.

Back to the mirror. Jab cross hook.

Jab cross hook.

You are a girl. What do you want to box for?

I suddenly see my mom in the reflection of the mirror. I feel her energy of being insignificant and dismissed. She had 12 kids and died at the age of 45.

I feel insignificant and dismissed. I feel the oppression of all women.

Slip. Duck.

Weave.

Jab cross hook.

Stop beating yourself up, Eliza! Keep practicing!

Build yourself up and learn to love yourself while living your life well, in honor of your mom, who did not get the chance.

You are all heart. When the pain hits, the plans do not change.

Keep breathing, keep healing.

You are powerful. You matter.

With your great strength,

you can show other women they have great power too.

Keep healing, keep practicing.

Keep working, Eliza. We are rising.

Jab cross hook upper.

You are killing it, Eliza! What are you trying to kill, Eliza?

Are you afraid to die, or are you afraid to truly live?

You have great gifts.

You must learn how to live with them in this world, even if they're different.

It's okay to be different.

You believe in the invisible energy of all times; you believe in magic.

Jab. Slip.

Uppercut.

Light on your toes!

What is your worth? What is your life's work worth?

What matters? What is the matter?

You have already died from cancer at 35.

You know what it means to come back to life and bring more gifts.

Keep breathing. Keep fighting for life.

No fear here, no fear here.

You got this.

Now go hit the bag. Release your tension.

Heal your wounds and fight for what you think matters most.

Bring real love and magic into this world.

Work that bag, don't let that bag work you. Work through the pain. Do not live your life through your wounds.

Get back to the light. Let the light be what heals those wounds. Light. Fast.

Hits. Power!

I'm out of breath. My body is exhausted from its work. I lay down on the cold, hard floor. I feel complete, whole. I'm filled with the energy of all time and people. Sweat turns into steam that rises from the top of my head as it settles.

My breathing slows down and becomes deeper. Peace comes over me. I suddenly see this lit ball of life in my hands. It's glowing; it's my life force. I marvel at its supernatural magic. This is my energy. This is what I've been preserving my whole life, and I will never extinguish the light from it.

My questions are the answers themselves.

What matters most and what I will make into matter. I am fully present.

This is the gift. It's simple but not simple-minded.

I am ready to offer this to the world.

I rise, stand tall in my true power, ready to train the people.

It's still early in the morning; the sun is now bursting its way through.

Several people start to walk down the alley. They, too, are being pulled to their personal power. Their eyes are still sleepy and start to open in their search for what they are seeking. They listen to their hearts and let the vibrational beat of all hearts lead them to the door.

"Good morning, Wolfie. How are you, Lamb? What's up, Doc?

Hi, 11:11."

Most of my clients have nicknames, and I have memorized their phone numbers by heart. I'm committed to making real connections while having human contact. My sober eyes look deep into theirs. I see them. I am here—heart forward.

My biggest muscle is my heart, and it greets them first thing.

I give them a strong hug; I know the journey they've been on.

They open the door to our spiritual playground. The place is packed; I wonder if I'm able to play with so many others at one time because I was raised with a team of heroes: my siblings. Here we can hold the opposites. Pain and joy, work and rest, weakness and strength, darkness and light, male and female. This is our practice. It takes repetition after repetition to build our practice into practical life.

We are spiritual scientists practicing our method over and over again until we've built a foundation of trust through self. No one can do the workout but them, but they don't have to do it alone. My plan is loose, it stays new, and I allow it to evolve naturally.

I hold the boxing mitts for them now. It's time they see their true power in their work. Part of what's driving them is their pain. They move through the awkwardness of their new practice.

Their hits are powerful, their truth is clumsy.

Their voices are weak but get stronger as they learn to speak. They are now my teacher; they show me what brave looks like.

It's like physics; they continue with curiosity to see what they'll discover by striking fiery hit after hit. I'm a conductor, a conduit of light. I become their mirror and reflect their pain and power back to them. I'm their muse; I dare them to give me all that they've got. I scare the shit out of them while asking them what their truth is.

My vision is clear; there is a special harmony of sensitivity and strength that allows them to fully show up.

"Give me all your power!" "Is that all you've got?"

"Go deeper!"

"Stay in your base."

"Show me what you're made of." "Make a name for yourself." "You matter."

"Go hit that bag. Hit it until you don't see the other person's face on it anymore. Go deeper. Get to yourself. It's your turn. Bring yourself back to life."

"Rise!"

"Rise!"

"Power!"

For the next part of their practice, I lead them through a cross-training program. They build a relationship with their body as they endure pain, much like the ecstasy and agony of giving birth. The biology of breaking down muscle fibers is a birthing similar in nature. We do a signature workout called Chance. I named it after my son.

The clock is set.

"Eight, nine, ten. . .and we go!"

Work.

Pain.

Gain.

"Finish strong!"

Most do not make it, but they know sometimes it takes five years to complete a workout. Their hard work is R-E-S-P-E-C-T, and they find out what it means to me. They are now lying on the floor, their hearts beating out of their chests. They feel like they almost died, but now feel more alive than they have ever felt.

They lie with their arms spread, hands wide open, and are now more connected to their breath, realizing this is what led them through the workout. Their body has been exhausted of all its armor, and they feel completely open. They can allow something deeper to come in.

It's now my turn to use this inlet to speak to what matters most.

This is our house.

This building we are in used to be the 22nd Liquor Store.

It is now Boxing is for Girls.

We are drinking from a different kind of spirits.

☥HE 𝕸EDICINE

I pull out my spiritual readings. Scrappy, the street cat, our spiritual advisor, saunters in as he feels the energy has shifted. He purrs and rubs his healing vibrations up against you. You pet him. He heals you. You let him.

Today, I speak to you about death.

I prepare you for your deathbed. I begin with your breath. I explain to you that your breath is the first and last thing you will do, and it is oftentimes the thing that is most ignored during your life.

I present the questions:

"What will you bring with you when you go out into the world?"
"What will you make into matter?"

You know a little bit about death now because you just survived the workout.

I remind you to face your fears so you can start truly living.

The Earth is the heart of the cosmos.

You're now more conscious of your ability to lead with your heart and put feelings back into life. You know we're not machines.

Strength comes from being vulnerable.

I know the undertaking and incredible responsibility of being a spiritual warrior.

I am this. What you see in me, you, too, are it. We are one.

I stick to my formula 1 + 1 = One.

As I run home, the crystals become the grid to life. I go over my day and go through my magical tool belt checklist.

Time is relative. Healing does not take time. Healing takes healing.

I heal myself and simultaneously, I heal others.

The street I'm running on becomes expansive and turns into my quantum field. Suddenly, I see my past self, and I say thank you to her for the innocence and purity in her power to stay committed to love while she endured all the pain. I see my present self and say, "You are doing it; you are carrying the lessons. You're making transformations; all this pain was not in vain, and I wouldn't take it away for anything." This is the very reason why I can hold the mitts for a six-foot-eight, 400-pound heavyweight champion who is eating himself to death, and I don't get hurt. I'm a shapeshifter; I become all energy. Mine, his, and of all times.

In the quantum, I can connect to all the great teachers who've passed. I become this unstoppable force of infinite wisdom and power. This is where I hold the hand of the dead. My future self reaches her hand towards my present self, and I take it and say, "Let's go! I trust you. I am home."

Movement is medicine; stillness is pure magic.

I lay my body down to rest and restore. I quiet my mind.

I drop into my sacred heart space, my soulmate.

I feel eternal love living here, where everything is okay.

I start to rest, I sleep soundly, peacefully, I keep my dreams awake.

My subconscious plays out the stories of the wounds again, my healing continues.

I also receive prescient messages that I will continue to integrate.

I'm awakened by an alarm. BAM! Still, I rise.

I begin with the end in mind. I do it all over again.

As I leave the studio to go home, I pause in gratitude at the purple eight-foot steel cross lit on the building. Creativity has always been a part of my healing process. I created this art piece in honor of Anna, Jesus' grandmother. The symbolism is a reminder of my dedication to light conception. I also feel the energy of my great-grandmother, Kissiah. She donated land for a church and cemetery, still standing today and where she is laid to rest. These two women I deeply know but have never met. Most of what I know I never had to be taught. It's in my very cellular makeup, in my blood, in my genes. I draw from the source of their strength and thank them for making my life into an answered prayer.

My medicine is my decision.

In my decision is my commitment. In my commitment is my plan.

In my plan is my heart.

In my heart is my pain.

In my pain is my power.

Connect with Eliza James at:

Website: https://boxingisforgirls.com/

Instagram: https://www.instagram.com/boxingisforgirls/

Facebook: https://www.facebook.com/BoxingIsForGirls

MOVEMENT IS MEDICINE, STILLNESS IS PURE MAGIC.

~ ELIZA JAMES

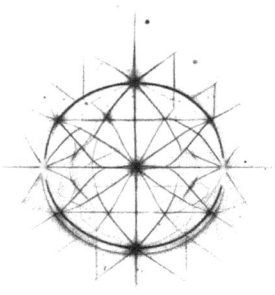

Chapter 5

DRAWING A BLANK

Redesigning Yourself, Your Thoughts, and Your Inner Dialogue
Rachelle Golding

YOU ARE ONLY EVER AT YOUR WORST
THE FIRST TIME YOU TRY SOMETHING NEW.
~ UNKNOWN

𝔐𝔶 𝔖𝔱𝔬𝔯𝔶

I remember thinking to myself as I spoke to Brian, my manager at the time: *Why did I have to open my mouth? Why couldn't I just lie down and take it? Was I being emotional and irrational? Not really. She had it coming.*

Releasing an audible sigh and rubbing my eyes, I thought, *I probably did it because I wanted her to suffer, to be in just as much pain as I was in.*

Bringing myself back to the present conversation, I heard Brian asking if I was sure I wanted to follow through with my formal complaint about the warehouse supervisor, Fiona. He advised me that it would become part of both our employee records and once entered, there would be no rescinding of my complaint. I recall saying, "Yes, I'm sure," as I felt the lump in my throat finding its resting place in the pit of my stomach.

Oh God, Rachelle, you're in deep shit now! I kept telling myself this as I attempted to keep the tears from flowing and my voice from shaking.

Brian then asked me to go over what happened the day prior to ensure there was a proper record of the event. Still feeling very raw and heartsick, I contemplated the rolling sensation of nausea.

Am I feeling sick because I don't want Brian to think less of me or because I know I am in trouble?

Giving my head a shake, I was touching on something so tender, coupled with the unhealthy compulsion to ensure everyone liked me. *Now isn't the time to be a self-reflective dummy.* My stress-triggered system was going into shutdown mode. With a trembling hand, I wiped away tears I didn't give permission to fall. *When did I start crying again?*

Without realizing how long I paused, Brian chimed in to indicate he had spoken with Fiona the morning prior, letting her know I suffered a grave family loss of three relatives in a house fire overnight, and as such, the schedule was changing to have me work the sales floor rather than in the warehouse.

Thankful for the prompt, I began recounting how I had been left to myself most of the day and it wasn't until closer to the end of my shift that Fiona paged me to call the warehouse. I recited the conversation between Fiona and me after the page:

"I need you in the warehouse now!" Fiona barked through the phone.

Emotionally exhausted and physically depleted, I sighed, "Okay, I will finish up with the last of the stock that I have, then I will head back."

"No! You will come here now." Fiona growled through the receiver.

With apprehension growing in my chest and ringing in my ear, I barked back, "No. I will finish with the stock, and then I will head to the warehouse."

As I recapped the conversation to Brian, I vividly remember the creeping sensation of foreboding, like that of a looming storm, while on the phone with Fiona. From the moment I heard her voice to the abruptness of her hanging up on me mid-sentence. I had begun mentally preparing myself for the fight I knew was coming.

She's going to start yelling at me; I just know it. What am I going to do? I should go hide in the bathroom. No, she will just hunt me down regardless of where I try to hide. I should yell right back at her, but I don't want to cause a scene. What should I say?

I went on to explain how, after the conversation, I made my way back to where I was working with tightness blooming in my chest. I finished with the last stock when I felt a hand grip the back of my arm. I recalled what Fiona said through gritted teeth, "I said to come back to the warehouse. Now." She then gripped my arm tighter and began to pull me in the direction of the warehouse. I remarked to Brian that it took significant effort, but I managed to wrench my arm free. At that moment, I felt a flood of adrenaline wash through my body. I saw red; I was ready for war.

I told Brian what I was thinking on the walk back to the warehouse.

How dare she touch me! What right does she have to invade my space? Un-fucking believable! Rachelle, just breathe. Try to remain calm. There is no point in making the situation worse than it already is. No, fuck that! She shouldn't have grabbed me like that.

I deliberately kept the less-than-work-appropriate thoughts out of my conversation with Brian. I remember feeling so small, ashamed, and disappointed in myself when I recounted how the conversation with Fiona went in the warehouse.

"How dare you be so disrespectful. When I order you to do something, your role is to listen!" Fiona snarled.

"Me being disrespectful. That is hardly the case here, Fiona," I replied. I tried to continue speaking, remaining as calm as I could, only to have her speak over me,

"Oh yes, it is. I'm the warehouse supervisor, which makes me your superior. You listen to me," she spat, and continuing, she asked, "What is your problem with me?"

With my cheeks burning and my heart pounding, I screamed, "Fiona, you're a bitch! No one likes you." As the words left my lips, the bloodthirsty warrior who walked into the warehouse disguised as Rachelle took her shot. We both stood stunned in silence, staring at one another, not believing the fierce words that escaped my lips.

At this point in the conversation with Brian, I took ownership of my part in the conflict. As I wiped away yet more rogue tears, I thought: *Well, there you go, you are in deep shit now. He now knows you called her a bitch. Fuck, I'm probably going to get reprimanded as bad or worse than Fiona.*

I told him I tried to remove myself from the situation by leaving for the day. However, Fiona was insistent on engaging further in the conflict, continuing to yell insults at me, all the while blocking my only exit. Terrifying thoughts flooded my mind, feeling like a caged and panicked animal attempting to flee its captor. *I need out! I can't breathe! I need air! Oh God, I'm trapped!* I continued to explain that I had to physically remove her from in front of the door in order to escape.

I felt incredibly distraught knowing that until that point in my life, I had never been so angry as to lose my cool in that fashion, to spew something so deliberately venomous at another person. It was shortly after this incident (and much to my relief) that I was transferred to another store location in my hometown of Cranbrook, British Columbia. It was back in Cranbrook where I found a posting that read: *"The Ascension Handbook: How to Navigate your Spirit in this Human Experience."* It was as if the Universe heard the yearning within my soul when I read the posting, answering with smooth tones, letting me know I was on the right track. The moment I read those words, I knew my life was never going to be the same.

Little did I know what a magical, miraculous, and wonderful journey of self-discovery it would send me on, and what amazing lessons, growth, and introspection it would unfurl within me. I didn't know how profoundly the ever-evolving teachings would impact my perception of what it means to truly listen, reflect, and understand inner dialogues, as well as what it means to be an observer of our inner conversations. I would learn to explore the teachings of self-discovery and make sense of the conversation in my head during the storm I had weathered, named Fiona.

ꝒHE ꝳEDICINE

My dearest reader,

I commend you for the strength to hold yourself in a space that'll surely crack you open. I commend you for appreciating the beauty of being raw and vulnerable, opening yourself up to allowing a deep healing process to begin. As well, I'd like to extend my gratitude to you for reading my story and for holding space for me while I shared this triggering ordeal. I thank you for taking the leap with us into this sacred container, which is this book.

Take a moment to listen to what kind of conversation you're having with yourself right now, at this very moment. Where are your thoughts taking you, and what type of physical reaction are you having in your body? Do you feel tension anywhere in your body? What did my story trigger in you? Are your thoughts now racing, or are they circling around a singular issue? Are you obsessing over a person, project, or situation you had no control over? What about your breathing? Is it shallow and quick? Now dip down into your heart space by straightening your back and taking three big, slow lung-expanding breaths. Listen to how quiet and calm it is here. Take another three big, expansive breaths. How does your body feel now? Do you still feel that tension, or has it eased? Simply observe.

Let us now travel to where we can gain a meaningful understanding of the relationship within ourselves. The personal abode I speak of within is a sacred place that no other person can hold captive. I speak of our heart space, the very center of our physical body. In chakra work, I believe the heart space is where the dense physical energy centers twirl and blend with the spiritual energy centers. It's in our heart space that, when opened and attuned to a higher vibration, leads to miraculous things. It's in this place that we can flesh out all that doesn't serve, creating a blank canvas to redesign ourselves and giving way to a shift in the frequency of our inner dialogue.

It's an odd concept, the idea that we all have an inner monologue happening that can manifest itself into the physical world. For many, myself included, it's typically a fear-based tug-of-war. Subsequently, it brings down our frequency to a much denser level. The question is, at what point did we allow ourselves to become slaves to its barrage of negativity and just accept it? When did we allow this negative little beasty, which I will refer to as Ego, to run so rampant? So constant is the chatter that over time it erodes us and can bring about episodes of anxiety and depression. The source of Ego is complex and can come from different experiences we've accumulated over our lifetime, and it'll look different for all of us.

The source of Ego can be any traumas, rejections, or concessions we've made with ourselves. To explore the depths to which the Ego has gone, it's important that we go into our heart space. This gives us the opportunity to hold ourselves in a safe container and to practice quieting the mind. By holding space for ourselves, we can then work towards the next step in our healing journey. The next step is being an observer of our inner dialogues, a stalker of ourselves, if you will. This means we must watch our thoughts without judgment or animosity.

When we take the position of a stalker in our inner dialogue, it's incredible what patterns of fear-based thoughts are caught. Fearful thinking could resemble thoughts like: There are so many incredible contributing authors to this book. I am not *good enough to be among them. Or, I don't have anything to offer; why bother?* Those are exactly the thoughts I had floating around while writing this. However, it presented a wonderful opportunity to drop into that heart space, to catch those thoughts, examine them at length, and release them without judgment. The ability to recognize this unhealthy train of thought is important because it stops the cascading effect of self-doubt paralysis. It offers me the room to shift my perception of how I view myself versus how I think the world perceives me. The practice I describe above may appear on the surface to be an easy task, but as the saying goes, it is easier said than done.

Being our own heart space stalker takes work. It's like any other muscle in the body. It requires care and attention to remain flexible. For our heart space to remain healthy and perform effectively, it must be exercised regularly to reach a higher vibrational level. Unlike traditional exercises for the body, attuning your heart space can take on many different consciously created daily practices. It could be journaling snips of the inner dialogues that occurred throughout the day, visualizations, meditation, connecting with like-minded people, or it could even be as simple as small acts of kindness.

My favorite way to keep the heart space in shape is with meditation. For me, meditation is a quiet walk out in nature with my dogs. Another way is to keep my child-like sense of wonder alive, stopping to admire a neat rock or finding dinosaur shapes amongst the clouds. Most important of all has been finding my tribe. To be among people willing to meet me at my level but push me just that little bit outside of my comfort zone, all the while respecting my boundaries.

The beauty of creating daily practices is that over time, they become unconscious, positive habits. It becomes easier to take a step back and observe the conversations we have within ourselves, to recognize thoughts that do not serve any purpose but create fear and anxiety. These positive habits we construct allow for deeper exploration of the traumas, rejections, or concessions we've made with ourselves. By holding ourselves in a place of love, we can be curious and open while exploring, without fear of re-traumatizing. It creates a foundation for you to build a healthier version of yourself. To catch yourself when you begin to allow old habits to creep back in.

So, what does all this mean for you, my dearest reader? Where do we go from here? Well, that's the beauty of this journey. It's yours to make of it what you wish. My words are yours now to mold and shape into what resonates deepest with you. They may be the launch pad that shoots you into a previously unexplored universe, or perhaps they will slip in and out of your consciousness like a gentle stream trickling down the mountainside. Either path is no more right or wrong than the other. Do not be discouraged if it's difficult at the beginning. These practices take time to hone. Always remember that you are only at your worst the very first time you try something new.

Rachelle Golding is a Canadian Rocky Mountain goddess. She is a loving wife to her high school sweetheart and fur-mother to two rambunctious canines and three mischievous felines. She is a court clerk with the Court Service Branch, a sector within the British Columbia Government. She is actively involved as a member of a multitude of health and wellness committees within the Court Service Branch organization. She walks in both the corporate world and the spiritual world with ease. Rachelle is a dedicated Reiki Master through the Usui System of Natural Healing. Her work with Angel has allowed her the honor of being one of the first priestesses initiates of the Nina Songo, Fire Heart Mystery School. As well, Rachelle is a practicing physical medium who believes when Spirit comes knocking, it's time to get rocking. With her zest for life and thirst for continued healing, she brings a ray of sunshine to every encounter.

Contact with Rachelle:

Instagram: @etherealpearls

Facebook: https://www.facebook.com/etherealpearls

BEING OUR OWN HEART SPACE STALKER TAKES WORK.
IT'S LIKE ANY OTHER MUSCLE IN THE BODY.

~RACHELLE GOLDING

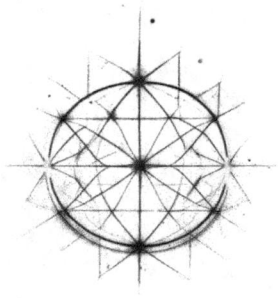

Chapter 6

THE FORGOTTEN SELF

How to Remember Her

Daphne Paras, MSEd

𝕸𝖞 𝕾𝖙𝖔𝖗𝖞

I was lying in the firm hotel bed, alone, with thoughts racing through my mind: *Am I truly dying? Will I see my girls again? I am so glad I got the medical evacuation insurance. Just hang on until one o'clock. You've got to make it to one.*

One o'clock came and the door opened. Silently, he went to the bathroom and then to the safe to check his iPad. Standing there, he read his emails, not even noticing my presence in the room.

What the fuck? Where are my children? Did you actually leave them alone at a pool in Mexico? Are you going to come and see me before I die?

I felt my blood pressure rising. Suddenly, I felt alive again.

I shouted with an energy I didn't even know I had, "What the fuck is wrong with you? I don't have a friend on Earth that wouldn't come straight to my bedside."

Flustered, he stared blankly at me.

The heartbreak and the anger—those moments—brought me back to life that day.

For the next three weeks, the tears I held in for so long streamed like a steady flowing river. The awakening was happening. Everything I held in and pretended was okay surfaced like an erupting volcano.

What the hell happened that day at Coba? What spirits woke me? What Universal powers are at play?

It started just like every other family vacation I planned, at least two weeks away to coerce my husband into spending time with his family. Beautiful pictures were taken of us all looking perfectly happy, with coordinated outfits, excursions, and everything seamlessly planned and executed.

We had never ventured to the pyramids before. I negotiated one family vacation a year. The rest of the trips were girls only. I convinced myself this was just fine and felt immense gratitude for traveling the world with my daughters.

We started out early to beat the heat, but by the time we reached the pyramid at Coba, the sun was scorching. We finally reached the top, and I knew we'd have to come back down soon, as there was no shade. It felt like we climbed up next to the sun. We peered over the edge. *Oh fuck, that is really steep!* I assured them we could do this, and carefully, step by step, backward, we navigated our way down.

Safe.

We were safer than I thought. We were protected. Looking back, I know the ancients were with me; I know they knew there was something much greater for my life and purpose, and they sure brought it.

I made a promise that I'd never put my girls through a divorce. I wouldn't let them experience the pain I did as a child. Then there was one moment, and it arrived on my doorstep like a ton of bricks: *What if one of them comes to me at almost 40, crying, in despair, telling me they were so lonely and in a loveless and sexless marriage?* A veil lifted; I'd be responsible, as that's the only example I've ever shown them. Once I saw that vision, I could not unsee it.

No more. We either change our marriage, or we end it.

If I had enough courage to really look at myself, I wouldn't have recognized who I had become. I had forgotten an entire self, completely buried her away to protect her.

Those tears? I couldn't stop them; I couldn't hide them; they were determined. I surrendered, over and over again. It felt like the ultimate act of vulnerability.

I had to pick the girls up at their mini-school and see the other moms, "Yes, I'm okay, maybe finally okay. I think I just held them in for too long." Everyone seemed to understand. Some joined me, others hugged me, and some confided their deepest secrets to me.

I had dinner plans with a friend and I didn't cancel. "I have these tears that just want to flow, and I can't stop them, so if you are okay with that, we can keep our plans." He sat next to me in my car, just being with me as I drove, and let those tears run.

I didn't judge them; I didn't question them. I allowed them. There was nothing else I could do. They trained me quickly.

I barely saw my husband; his travel kept him away for almost the entire three weeks, which was common. I had little faith we could shift. He couldn't be with the tears anyway; he didn't know me that way. No one did.

I started opening up to a few close friends about the despair I had denied. My perfect life wasn't so perfect. Up until this point, I couldn't see it; I wouldn't see it. I was determined to make my life work the way I believed it should.

Another dear friend gifted me a session with an intuitive. The first sentence she spoke after "hello" was, "This separation will be a good thing."

What? Who told her this? Oh, my friend had to have filled her in. Nope. The guides spoke to her. Okay, lady, you have my full attention. "Harness your goddess energy," she said calmly, "that is your key." Well, great, what the fuck does that mean?

I began searching for answers. I needed wisdom, a roadmap, guidance, call it whatever you like. I was a sponge trying to soak up anything I could to soothe my soul, to give me an explanation of what was happening to me and how to move through it.

I was in the laundry room of a ski rental in Colorado. I left the girls and my dad upstairs. I was having an epic release. My dad couldn't be with my tears either. I was getting it out on the phone with a friend, and he told me, "This is your return to Uranus, your midline. When you're not living in accord with your higher purpose, the Universe will conspire to change it. That's all."

That's all? Well, this makes perfect sense, but can the Universe be a bit gentler on me? No, of course not. It tried the gentle route, the knocking on my door, and I didn't listen. Or I couldn't hear it.

My husband discovered some text messages while I was away. There was a man I had several dinners with, with my husband's consent and knowledge. It was during that time that I really discovered he didn't care what I did or with whom I did it.

Throughout our marriage, about once a year, I broke down in despair. I pleaded, "Why won't you touch me? What is wrong with me? I need touch. I need sex. I need affection." It didn't make a difference.

We tried counseling. I tried being the perfect wife. The house was spotless, the girls were well-behaved, and I was the prettiest I could be.

I even asked for an open marriage once. I thought that if I could get one need met, I could survive staying. I created stories: *Maybe he doesn't respect me staying home, maybe he doesn't like my post-baby body, maybe he's having an affair. . .maybe, maybe, maybe.*

In those texts he found, there was some PG-13 flirting. He also read my words, "I will not cheat on my husband, it's not who I am, but I'd be interested in exploring dating you if and when we separated."

The fear kicked in full throttle for him, and he told me he'd fight to the ends of the Earth to save our marriage. *Okay, let's try this!*

I returned from Colorado almost exactly four weeks after climbing Coba, to the man I fell in love with—attentive, interested, and sexual.

The next 14 months became the most amazing, challenging, and heartbreaking time of my life. He connected, and then completely disconnected, ten times over the course of those 14 months. Each time the connection period shortened, each time my heart was ripped open deeper.

My heart, could you still be broken even more? Or are you breaking open so deeply that you can expand more than you ever have?

It was as if a light switch was flicked on and off. On, he was the man I fell in love with. Off, he was the cold, disconnected stranger who didn't even see me walk by him fully naked.

We went through three different therapists. He didn't see a problem. I spent so much life force energy wondering about him not being able to meet my needs. *Is he unable? Or just unwilling?* At the end of the day, it didn't matter. My needs were so far from being met.

I was attending workshops for myself and gaining certifications to embody my goddess energy and teach others how to do so. I became a work in progress, rather than a pretty finished product. I owned it. I talked about my journey, my despair, and my heartache.

We returned to Hawaii, where he asked me to marry him again. I couldn't. I compromised on a commitment ceremony where I spoke of commitments I could honor, being the best me possible, doing the work, and being accountable.

That night at dinner, he leaned over to me and whispered in my ear, "I forgot to say my commitments, didn't I?" With the familiar heartbreak, I replied, "Yes, you are correct." I wish I could say I was surprised.

The next morning, we were at breakfast. The waitress had the name of his ex-wife. It sparked a conversation about their wedding. The girls and I were learning about his previous life. When I pressed for the location, he reminded me we'd been there together, just five months before. In fact, I was in such awe of the hotel that I exclaimed, "Could you imagine getting married here?!"

I circled back, "When I said, 'could you imagine getting married here,' and you said 'yeah,' I didn't realize it was because you actually did get married there."

"Daph, I honestly didn't even connect the two until just now."

I believed him. He was that disconnected. Our third therapist believed he had an addiction to disconnection. *Well, that certainly explains a few things.*

You see, I remember every place I've ever kissed someone, and definitely every bigger moment. But we were different. I lived in a place of connectedness and vulnerability, with my heart open, or at least I tried.

I took my rings off that day and never put them back on. I asked him to move out when we returned home.

Oh my heart, my brave and terrified heart. What have I done?

In a matter of days, I helped him find an apartment. A shaman I worked with described the energy of his coming and going like a 747-jet taking off and landing. The jet took off, a cloud lifted from the house, and it never landed there again.

The next phase of work began—uncovering the depths of rejection and working through the healing process.

The first time I imagined being sexual with another human, my heart stopped. I was now months away from turning 40. I hadn't been sexually active with another since my 20s. The fear, the contraction, it was paralyzing.

What has happened to me? Where did that vibrant, sexual, confident woman go? It was as if I had completely forgotten an entire self. *How do I remember her?*

I started my own personal journey, Friday-night date nights, where I dated myself. I cooked a gourmet dinner for one, watched a scary movie, took a Zumba class, dove into sacred self-pleasuring, and sometimes did all of them!

Somewhere on this journey, I learned that when we sever our connection to our sexuality, we cut off our life force energy. Literally, as women, our womb space creates life. So many of us, from one sort of trauma or another, sever that connection. It made so much sense to me, and I realized how severing this connection was such a punishment to myself and the world around me. I was determined to repair it.

After all, when we're in alignment with our sexuality, we show up differently in the world; at the grocery store, as a mom, as a boss babe. You know the women I'm talking about—fully present in their bodies, with a certain confidence about them, aware of the intricacies that light them up. I wanted in on that!

I started with a very intentional self-pleasure practice, relearning my body as if I was brand new to her and she was brand new to me. I learned what she liked, what she felt like, and even what she looked like. I made peace with her, acknowledging the changes she had endured and the feats she had accomplished, loving her over and over again.

When the time felt right, I called in partners. I knew I needed my focus to be on my girls, and that the road ahead would be expansive and challenging. I had lovers who were gentle, amazing, and loving. Most of all, they accepted where I was on my journey, and celebrated me for it.

I continued facilitating workshops and grew my offerings. The more I spoke my truth, the more the collective healed with me.

As I learned of so many women who also severed their connection to their sacred sexuality, my flame grew for this underserved and rarely talked about phenomenon.

I set out to shift my mind, body, and spirit. My core belief is that each and every one of us is born with a set of gifts. Our job is to uncover those gifts and use them to better this world. As I grew further into alignment with my gifts, I felt all the support I needed. The Universe was cheering me on every step of the way. I woke up and asked, "What magic is going to happen today?" And the magic happened.

𝕿𝖍𝖊 𝕸𝖊𝖉𝖎𝖈𝖎𝖓𝖊

I developed many practices to thrive.

Return to your body. Surrender. Connect. Listen. Heal. Repeat. These were the words that I lived by.

My mind was busier than ever. Constantly trying to solve every possible dilemma. I felt like a crazy person. The controller in me was in charge, and the more I tried to control, the less control I felt.

Gratitude.

I wrote it on sticky notes and placed them all over my home, two still hang to this day.

I set up a gratitude reminder on my phone to alert me every 30 minutes of my awake hours. Whenever those bells would chime, no matter what I was doing or who I was with, I stopped, placed my hand firmly on my heart, and said at least one thing I was thankful for. When I was with others I simply asked, "Would you like to join me in a moment of gratitude?" The response was always an excited "Yes!" I trained myself. After a few weeks, when my disaster mind ran on and on, I could just stop, place my hand on my heart, and shift into my body. As I continued practicing shifting out of the fear from my mind into the magic of my body, my heart expanded.

Self-pleasure.

My sexuality was poorly neglected for far too long. It was as if I took the rejection from my husband and used it to punish myself. I completely internalized it and even convinced myself I wasn't a sexual being anymore. It took me some time to feel sexual and connected to my body again.

Starting with my breath, I create an orb of light, breathing it into my root chakra. On the inhale, I run it up the spine of my body and on the exhale, down the front, creating a loop. I use the light to clear any blockages and stagnant energy. From there to the sacral chakra, solar plexus, heart, throat, third eye, and finally the crown chakra. I spend as much time as I need to at each chakra, using my breath, and the orb of light to clear.

Each time, using my breath to take the orb all the way back down to my root chakra and loop it back up again.

I found it important to set up a sacred space and ritual for this. Sometimes just lighting a candle, other times starting with a bath and massaging delicious body butter into my skin with sensual music and essential oils diffusing.

Setting the intention to love and heal myself, to honor any and all feelings that would arise, to let go of any expectations, to have fun, and to be fully present.

I began to incorporate self-pleasure with this breathing and chakra clearing. Breast massage became an epic tool to open my heart. My breasts had an awakening of their own when they gave life to my daughters. Honoring and worshipping their power felt in total alignment with my goddess energy. I tried different toys to explore pleasure and different varieties of orgasms. A cervical orgasm? Yes, please!

Building up the pleasure as my breath moved throughout my body allowed me to be fully present in each chakra. I played with building that energy, then holding it as I reached the crown chakra, coordinating my climax with the crown, letting the energy explode from my head and into the Universe, and letting it rain back down onto my being–exquisite.

Return to your body. Surrender. Connect. Listen. Heal. Repeat—as many times over as you need.

Daphne Paras leads people by igniting the fire within them. She has found great satisfaction in facilitating corporate and private workshops, as well as one-on-one coaching. She excels at holding space and guiding people deep into the wisdom of their bodies, where she believes the magic happens. Daphne leads by example, often citing she is both the teacher and the student, always on a mission to learn and expand more.

She has learned how to go deeper within herself, and in turn take others deeper using tools such as breathwork, meditation, and a variety of guided practices. She is passionate about helping women identify where trauma lives in the body and using pathways to clear and heal it.

Her journey led her to design and invent The Seeker, a sacred self-exploration and pleasure tool. She is on a mission to remove the shame and guilt and normalize open conversation and communication around sexuality. As well as inspire living in pleasure!

Daphne facilitates workshops around empowerment, reclaiming your voice, sexuality, and returning to your authentic self. One of her favorite experiences for helping people be fully present in their bodies is Firewalking. Her work as a firewalk Master allows her to certify instructors and facilitate workshops guiding people into their fears and across 1800-degree coals.

Daphne believes one of the greatest honors and responsibilities she has is guiding her teenage daughters. With loving, open communication and connection, her goal is to help them thrive and live without shame or guilt.

She is in a conscious partnership with a man who is her perfect mirror and lights her up entirely. She rests in the safety of the divine masculine to hold for her in all the ways she has needed to heal and fully bloom.

Connect with Daphne:

Website: https://www.sacredseeker.com/

MY CORE BELIEF IS THAT EACH AND EVERY ONE OF US IS
BORN WITH A SET OF GIFTS. OUR JOB IS TO UNCOVER THOSE GIFTS
AND USE THEM TO BETTER THIS WORLD.

~ DAPHNE PARAS

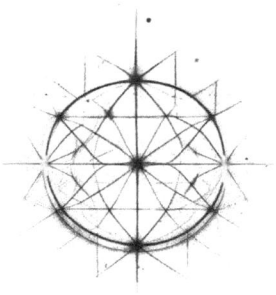

Chapter 7

THE SECRET OF HUMMING

Harnessing the Power of Your Voice for Personal Transformation
Bradford W. Tilden, CTM, MM, UWT

"IN THE BEGINNING WAS THE WORD,
AND THE WORD WAS WITH GOD,
AND THE WORD WAS GOD."

~JOHN 1:1

My Story

*In the beginning was the word. . .*I burst out laughing in the shower. Loud belly laughs. You know the type—the ones that make *your* sides hurt and make you gasp for breath. I was laughing because my spirit guides suggested I open this chapter with the above verse from the bible. It's the perfect verse in so many ways. It's a profound implication of the workings of manifestation, a reminder that we are God-like beings co-creating this shared reality and tells us sound is the key.

I didn't grow up religious, although I was raised Congregationalist. As a child, I didn't get the concept of having an intermediary between myself and the divine source of creation. I was wired differently, and because of certain unique experiences I had as a child, I became a seeker of spiritual truths at an early age.

I developed an authentic connection with the God of my understanding primarily through direct experiences. Great Spirit, as the natives put it, the "All," according to the ETs, and the Universe being my personal favorite, all speak of the same divine intelligence. Most importantly, I came to acknowledge that we ourselves are reflections and unique expressions of God.

"In the beginning was the word, and the word was. . .Hmmmm.

Hmmmm. Hmmmm." Or at least that is what it was for me.

These were the first sounds I made as I entered this world. I wasn't born crying. Instead, when they placed me in my mother's arms, I began to hum. Not only that, my mother will tell you how all the doctors and nurses gathered around to listen to the miraculous humming baby.

For years, I pondered what compelled me to hum as my first instinct upon entering this world. Was I simply content upon arrival? Was I giving my future self a signpost? Was I recreating the sensation of being in the womb? Was I intuitively counteracting the discordant buzz of the overhead fluorescent lighting? How would I know to do such a thing? What knowledge did I bring with me? What is this secret of humming?

I used to think it peculiar and interesting that I attracted an audience with my humming within minutes of my birth. Now it makes complete sense, given the career I've built. As a professional sound healer, people gather around me to listen and receive the healing sounds of my angelic and shamanic vocal toning, humming and all.

Even though I was born with this vocal note-to-self, this beautiful openness, I wasn't always this aligned with my gift of healing vocal expression. I, too, experienced trauma as a child that disconnected me from my power. I remember vividly the moment I began to doubt myself.

I was an unabashed, flamboyant young performer at seven years old. I loved to dance and sing along with my favorite songs. My song of choice at that time was *"Take My Breath Away"* by Berlin. I was being babysat by an older cousin. I was performing for her, swaying and singing with all my heart's content, lost in the reverie of sonic bliss, "Take my breath awaaaaay. . ."

When suddenly, I was snatched out of it by my cousin's sharp remark, "You're singing out of tune!" Maybe it wasn't intended to be harsh criticism, but her words pierced my heart and wounded my joy.

Was I singing out of tune? I didn't think so. It didn't sound like it to me. What if I've been singing out of tune this whole time and didn't realize it? I thought I was singing in tune!

These thoughts of self-criticism flooded my sensitive, impressionable mind. With one seemingly insignificant comment, the seeds of self-consciousness took root, and my joy of singing began to slip away.

Singing in public became tentative after that, and my world became unsure.

Not long after, I experienced another trauma that silenced my voice from all public consumption for years to come. It was the proverbial middle school musical. I was cast as the lead tenor in a light-hearted parody called "Hey, George" by Elizabeth Peach and Sally McBride about George the knight who goes to slay the last dragon. I had to sing a tenor solo in front of the entire student body. Nervousness doesn't even come close to the anxiety my peer-pressured pre-pubescent self-suffered before, during, and after that excruciating moment of torture. You see, the melody was written so there is a leap up whenever I had to sing "Hey—Geooooorge. . ." that went right into the top of my cracking vocal range. It was more terrifying and embarrassing for me than the real stage kiss I also had to give to the heroine later on, after I saved her, and that says a lot!

That was the last time I sang publicly for 12 years.

Privately, however, my voice was free and creatively thriving. My falsetto voice was a place I adored exploring any chance I got. I was, and am still, an opera diva in the shower. During church services, I sang the soprano line to the hymns even though my mother would elbow me in the ribs every time I did. I mimicked sounds with my voice, inspired by Michael Winslow from his scene in the 1987 movie *Spaceballs*.

I was fortunate to be born into a loud family. We all loved to scream, not in anger, but as a preferred means of communication. Instead of coming close to converse, we shouted to each other between two, and sometimes three, floors of our house. I also grew up surrounded by woods, where I spent much of my time after school. When I heard the faint cry of my mother's voice from deep within the forest, indicating dinner was ready, I shouted with all of my strength in response, indicating I received her call. This is significant because I naturally kept my voice full, with the diaphragm, the seat of power, engaged.

All of this and more became relevant once I discovered my voice as a healing tool. Upon reflection, I came to realize I developed and mastered the instrument of my voice my whole life, despite the public shaming I endured as a child. That is unique because many people shut their voices down. I work with clients who come to me with completely closed throat chakras, insecurities, low confidence, self-doubt, limiting beliefs, fear of self-assertiveness, etc., due to psychological and emotional traumas and childhood conditioning.

In retrospect, the first time I intentionally used my voice therapeutically was when I started mowing lawns for extra money when I was a young teenager, although I really didn't understand what I was doing at the time. Instead of using earplugs or listening to music in headphones, I hummed with the lawnmower motor. I would *listen* and *feel* the vibrations and harmonize with its dominant drone frequency. Having the language to describe it now, I was constructing a coherent resonant sonic field out of otherwise destructive noise, one that my body could easily assimilate. I did this naturally and intuitively, much like the day I was born, I imagine.

My experience was that I could not only tolerate the loud sound of the lawnmower, but I was also moved into a trance-like state of vibrational alignment with the sound, and was able to mow large lawns in a meditative state, feeling rejuvenated and energized afterward.

Today I don't have a lawn to mow. Instead, I harmonize in this way with my vacuum cleaner, my high-powered blender, and my favorite, my electric toothbrush. Humming a pitch that's in harmony with the strongest frequency of a motor will generate a coherent sonic field that's healthy for your body and energy. This is a secret of humming. Try it at home and write to me of your discoveries. I'd love to hear about them.

Growing up, I exhibited a highly developed musical aptitude. I begged my parents to give me piano lessons. It became apparent I was a prodigy. Playing the piano brought me the greatly needed outlet for my complex emotional expression, and I soon began composing original pieces. It also, unfortunately, became a source of intense performance anxiety, pressure, obsession with perfectionism, and rigidity of execution when performing publicly. God forbid I played the wrong note.

The pressure for me to win or place at competitions was nothing compared to the pressure I placed on myself when playing my original music in front of others. I was so hyper-critical of mistakes I'd made; I wasn't able to appreciate the beauty of my own music and performances. Despite my talent, I was a self-incarcerated prisoner to the notes on the page for many years.

One thing to mention, it was at those tedious piano recitals that I first learned to trace my finger around the rim of a water glass to make it hum. This was the tiny seed that would blossom into a profound awakening for me and the liberation from my musical imprisonment to follow.

In addition to music, my development was guided by unusual occurrences.

When I was very young, I had a recurring nightmare where I was being chased by a black puma. Each time, just as I leaped to safety, it slashed my back with its claws, and I woke up in pain. I later learned that this is an indication of shamanic initiation. In shamanic traditions, the shaman uses rituals and ceremonies to transform fear.

I believe I faced my first shamanic initiation at the age of 11. I started to feel an invisible presence in my bedroom that terrified me. I wouldn't go upstairs alone. The fear of this unseen presence went on for weeks until one day, I was sent to my room. I screamed and shouted for my parents to let me out because I was terrified of the presence in the room with me.

With no other options, I confronted my fear. I turned my back to the door and faced the presence. It immediately entered my solar plexus, and I was no longer afraid.

What just happened? I asked myself.

The presence was gone. I never sensed it again. Overnight, I became interested in the occult and esoteric studies, searching for answers. Within a few years, I was reading Carl Jung. Eventually, Dolores Cannon's work on soul integrations provided an explanation.

When I was a freshman in college, I woke one night to find a glowing angel hovering above my bed who proceeded to hand me a flaming sword. I later understood I was given the sword of truth by Archangel Michael. That was the first time I was visited by one of the Archangels.

These are a few examples of the many unique experiences, including more shamanic initiations, soul integrations, and angelic visitations, that helped shape my beliefs and guide me along my path.

But what was I to make of it all?

During my senior year, I repeatedly asked myself, "What's my purpose?"

And I repeatedly got the surprising answer, "To sing!"

How could that be? I don't sing. What does it mean? Is this metaphorical? This doesn't make any sense to me.

Around the same time, I started hearing a mysterious drone in my head. It sounded unlike any instrument I had ever heard. I was compelled to sing and harmonize with it in the shower. It was so alluring; I even composed a chamber piece for my senior thesis with a passage inspired by it. I orchestrated for the tones produced by circling around the rims of wine glasses because that was the closest sound to what I heard in my head. Little did I know I was experiencing clairaudiently what I would discover to be the sound of quartz crystal singing bowls.

From shamanic initiations to angelic visitations, to my cryptic purpose, and mysterious sounds in my head, I was being shown the way.

Each year, two graduating music majors are awarded a fellowship to stay on as either the assistant orchestral director or the assistant choral director. Having a background in piano, percussion, and cello, I naturally applied for the orchestral assistant position. To my surprise, I was offered the choral assistant position!

Suddenly, the message "to sing" made a whole lot of sense. I said "Yes!" to the opportunity.

With no experience, I found myself directing four choral groups and singing in three of them. Talk about an initiation! I also received a year of formal classical voice training. Interestingly, that teacher handed me a copy of Barbara Brennan's seminal work on energy healing, *Hands of Light,* out of the blue at our last lesson, saying, "I think this will come in handy for you in the future."

Receiving that book partially influenced my decision to attend school for massage therapy after completing my fellowship at Amherst College. That decision set in motion a series of probabilities that ultimately led me to enroll in a sound healing institute where I first encountered a quartz crystal singing bowl.

I can best describe the sensation as an opening, as if someone had unlocked a hatchway in my head and said, "Welcome home."

This is the sound that has been haunting me for four years!

Within two weeks, I manifested my own quartz singing bowl. My first instinct was to hum with it. When humming, my whole chest cavity would vibrate. I observed that when I hummed the exact same pitch, the physical vibrations inside me intensified. The secrets of humming once again began to reveal themselves to me.

Not limited to humming, I began to vocalize, to *'tone'* with the bowl. I became fascinated by the correlation of bodily sensations produced by the interaction of the sounds of my voice in relation to the pitch of the bowl. Through experimentation and exploration, I developed an entire realm of expression and discovery within the boundaries of my breath and body.

I found that uninterrupted toning for extended periods of time brought me to heightened states of consciousness, deep states of bliss, emotional release, healing, and inner peace. I developed self-mastery and incredible body awareness through the use of my breath and voice. To this day, I employ this simple life-management skill almost every day to clear my mind, emotions, and field to stay balanced and aligned.

Singing with crystal bowls emancipated me from the learned restrictions that rigid classical musical training had imposed upon me. I was at last liberated in my expression! What's best—no stage fright! It also helped me overcome performance anxiety when playing the piano in public. All of those earlier experiences in my life were contextualized, and their meanings became clear to me, and I had healed the trauma.

Toning also helped me to discover other gifts. While toning, I received the next pitch in my head and learned to sing channeled songs and chants. I started holding sound healing meditations and doing this in front of other people with amazing results!

It wasn't until I gave myself permission to fully express myself in public that the true magic of healing began manifesting amidst my audiences.

I could call in angels and indigenous spirits. I soon opened to channel them directly through my voice. I'd unlocked the secret of humming and self-actualized as a shamanic angelic sound healer.

The seeds of my healing transformation through self-discovery were planted in my first performance as that miraculous humming baby. Perhaps I wanted to remind myself and others of the one tool we all carry within us —our voices —and how simple it is to use.

Rediscovering the true power of my voice helped free me from limitations and restrictions in my personal life and career. Now I offer clients techniques for personal transformation using their voices as well. Allow me to share the secret of humming with you.

The Medicine

Here are a few simple exercises to help you start using your voice as a tool for managing stress and clearing stuck emotions. Try not to let self-criticism and self-consciousness prevent you from fully exploring the sound of your own voice. You can explore each of them independently for a length of time, switch it up, or just follow your innate sense of expression.

Find a private place where you can feel comfortable making sounds.

Inhale deeply, then audibly sigh on your entire exhale. Pay attention to the vibrations in your body. Repeat this two times. Pause. Notice how you feel.

Now inhale, then hum a pitch for the entire exhale. Place your hand on your chest to better feel the vibrations. Hum three times, exploring different pitches. Notice how different places inside you vibrate.

Pause. Notice how you feel.

Humming simulates the sensation of being in the womb. It's nurturing, calming, reduces anxiety, brings you back into your body, and grounds you.

Now you are ready to begin toning.

On the next exhale, produce and sustain the vowel sound "Oh" until the end of your breath.

Inhale slowly and completely and immediately exhale "Oh" again, two more times consecutively without interruption. Tone the same pitch each time.

Notice how you feel. This opens and expands your energy while clearing stress and releasing blocked emotions. It's that simple.

Now do the same three times with the vowel sound "Ah". This is a heart opener and can lift your mood and raise your energy.

Next alternate humming with "Ah" multiple times within a single breath. Do this three times. Focus on the changing inner sensations. Notice how much longer your exhale lasts.

Lastly, tone A-U-M (Ohm) three times, slowly transitioning between the vowels, closing on "M" as a hum. You are now embodying the sacred Sanskrit seed syllable for all creation, opening your heart, expanding your energy, and grounding within.

Notice how you feel.

Visit www.BradfordTilden.com to download a free toning track where you can practice the above exercises with me.

Bradford W. Tilden, MM, CMT, UWT is an internationally best-selling author, composer, pianist, cosmic shaman, and master intuitive vibrational healer specializing in sound, crystal, gemstone, and Universal White Time Healing. He's one of the pioneering UWT gemstone and energy healing teachers in North America. He graduated magna cum laude from Amherst College in 2002, attended the Globe Institute of Sound and Consciousness in San Francisco in 2006, and received a master's degree in music composition from UMASS, Amherst, in 2014.

Bradford founded the Lemurian School of Intuitive Natural Healing in 2008. The mission of LSINH (pronounced "listen") is to develop one's intuition while utilizing the power of sound and crystals to become an effective healer for oneself and the world. It's derived from the knowledge of the ancient Lemurian civilization, as revealed to him by his UWT crystal master guides, past life remembrance as a Lemurian priest-healer, and through his work with Lemurian seed crystals.

As a sacred sound ceremonialist, his music and live sound journeys are divinely orchestrated collaborations. Bradford vocally channels authentic angelic, galactic, and shamanic healing frequencies. Find his music on all the major streaming platforms. You can also support his music at https://bradfordwtilden.bandcamp.com

Bradford unearths the greatness in people through inspiration, education, and activation of the mastery within. Visit https://www.CrystalMusicHealing.com to learn more about UWT, LSINH, and all the remote healing services and products he offers, including spiritual upgrades. Contact him for music/sound healing commissions or to host a class. He will travel anywhere in the world to teach. Book a free 20-minute consultation here: https://calendly.com/crystalmusichealing/20min He would love to hear from you.

When he's not hiking or running around with his shirt off, you can find him playing the piano or talking to his crystals at home in Cheshire, CT.

Connect with Bradford:

LinkTree: https://linktr.ee/bradfordtilden

Facebook: https://Facebook.com/CrystalMusicHealing

Instagram: https://instagram.com/BradfordTilden

YouTube: https://youtube.com/MuseOfAquarius

LinkedIn: https://www.linkedin.com/in/bradfordtilden/

REDISCOVERING THE TRUE POWER OF MY VOICE HELPED
FREE ME FROM LIMITATION AND RESTRICTION IN MY
PERSONAL LIFE AND CAREER.

~ BRADFORD W. TILDEN

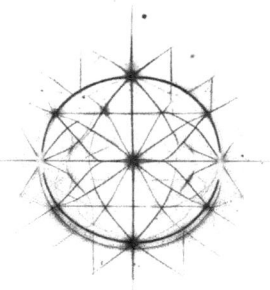

Chapter 8

THE DREAM THAT SAID HE'D DIE

The Truth Was, I Did

Angel Gold

𝕸y 𝕾tory

How am I going to do this alone? I can't do this! Don't leave me!

In June 2022, I had a full hysterectomy and one of the most epic shamanic deaths I've ever experienced.

It started with a dream that would forever change my acceptance of my psychic abilities, as this dream manifested in physical form weeks later.

My Dream

Raging white water, crashing against the cradling of Mother Earth,
shifting directions, rolling balls of fury,
spraying rainbow-filled droplets of water
as the river thrashes down the ancient, carved-out liquid trail.
The sun beats down, reflecting off the cool, misty spray,
drying the logs and branches hanging into and over the river.
He's lying face down, jammed in the logs, the water rushing over his lifeless body
As Pacha Mama calls him home.

Gasping for air, my eyes shoot open as my hand reaches for my heart.

My eyes fall upon my big lump of a husband, all tucked in, breathing peacefully beside me.

He's alive. You can breathe.

I repeat this to myself over and over until my heart comes back into a resting space.

I choose not to tell him. *It was just a dream, right?*

Two days later, he looks at his phone with his eyebrows furrowed. "The whitewater rafting group says the river may be too dangerous to be on; a man has been missing for a couple of days now."

My mind goes into overdrive. *You must tell him! His life may be in danger! Someone just died on that river, and now you're going to let your husband go?*

My truth is, I can't control anyone's actions.

I can provide him with the information I received, and he can then make better-informed decisions. So, I choose to share my dream and request that he stay acutely aware of his surroundings. "If you get a red light when you get out there, you should call it, don't go." He agrees.

The surgeon's office calls; there's been a cancellation. *Do I want to have my hysterectomy next week?*

The captain will leave three days after my surgery if I move it up.
Am I okay with healing by myself?
Oooh, this is a big test, but should I even have to test myself at this point?
Is it fair to ask him to stay home when this group planned their trip for months?

Nah, I got this; it'll be fine!

Surgery day arrives. I'm tucked into my room; my husband has gone for the night, and I'm ready for dreamland. Screeching pierces my ears as desperate words form in a female voice: "Get away from me!"

"Get him out of here!"

Wailing, scurrying carts, the shuffle of feet, squeaks off the floor as humans shift in the hallway.

More deep voices arrive, with more shuffling as she continues to wail.

I can't stand it. What's going on out there?

My heart is pounding in rhythm with the throbbing in my womb space.

Adrenaline pumping through my veins shoots me out of bed to peer out from behind my flimsy curtain door. My swollen eyes are bombarded with a handful of black security vests as an energetic wall of searing trauma hits me. Shell shock hurls me back into my bed as the panic attack sets in.

I can't breathe, I can't breathe, I can't breathe. Nurse!

The next three days and nights are filled with dream after dream of the violence I already processed in this lifetime. Experiencing it on a whole new level, drug-induced, the excruciating pain aligns with the excruciating experiences and creates new trauma.

While my husband packs for his trip to perhaps face his own death.

The morning arrives.

He stands in the doorway of our bedroom, looking down at me. In my hazy space, I try to memorize every particle of his being I can. My heart shatters as I hear what I feel is the last "goodbye" seep from my moist lips as tears fall down my cheeks.

I must let him go. This is the shaman's way.

Attach on the inhale and detach on the exhale.

How am I going to do this alone? I can't do this! Don't leave me!

Can't you see, I need you right now?

He must choose. It's not your choice. You must let him go.

As I hear the truck pull away, deafening stillness enters the room, and something dies inside me.

The next 24 hours become a trauma/drug-induced space of out-of-body experiences.

I will myself to go into intentional, deep meditation.

As usual, I end up on the top of the Pyramid of the Sun in Teotihuacán. I'm reminded we're all one, and I have access to him and his energy, whether it's on this physical plane or not. I've already experienced this phenomenon with others, and I did choose to marry a fire captain.

Every day, he puts his life on the line. Every day.

He's at work right now as I type this letter. He may not come home tomorrow.

This is the life I chose. This is the story I created.

If he dies on the river, he'll die doing something he loves with so much passion. He's a water element, after all.

Just because your head receives information does not mean your body receives it until you teach it. You can parrot the information out of your mouth all you want, but how will you react when it happens, for realsies?

This wonderfully crafted experiment the Universe and I dance through, sheds light on mental triggers around domestic violence and abandonment. My physical body writhes in excruciating pain from ripped out female parts and is inundated with drugs my brain can't process.

This leads to a lethal combination and perfect storm when I'm left with only one day of help, then left isolated at home to heal alone.

The contents of the pill bottle accidentally spill into the palm of my hand as I reach for my next dose.

Stillness permeates the room as I have a chat with the Universe.

I'm done playing this way.

If you want to use me as your vessel to serve humanity, I need a softer way.

I have succeeded in my pursuits in this lifetime; I have nothing to prove to anyone, and I just watched my soulmate, my warrior, walk out the door.

I'm putting down my sword.

I absolutely could leave this Earth right now and be so proud of what I've already accomplished within, healing my ancestral lines in this lifetime.

I'm not scared of you, Angel of Death.

If you want me to stay and be in service,
I want a new storyline filled with joy and service.
So mote it be.

Clearly, I chose life at that moment, and my work began anew.

Step one was a doozy.

I chuck out the poison the surgeon gave me. *I birthed children with no drugs; I can do this, too.*

I create new ways to process pain and trauma, as my "go to" is big releases through big, ugly snot cries. "Get it all out at once and it's done." Turn on the firehose and release.

Yeah, that doesn't work when you can't breathe!

I adjust my breathwork and figure out how to release the energy without the big explosion, as all my intercostal rib muscles scream. I didn't know they were going to blow my insides up like a balloon and stretch me to my limits from the inside in that surgery.

I feel like I'm being beaten with a well-tuned baseball bat.

How do I process trauma without crying?

Without expanding my ribcage? No deep breaths.

I keep my breath turtle-slow and steady while my adrenals fire like I'm about to die, because that's what it feels like.

I spend hours recapitulating whatever timeline shows up and hours a day with each of my inner children who still have residual hurts left to clean. I pay attention to what still has energy left in it and what can be completely cut and transmuted.

I go to sleep and wake up crying. I hold and remind my body we aren't releasing that way this time; we're trying it this other way.

The captain is gone for a week with no contact.

When he does choose to check in, I'm shocked at what he has to say. "You were right." With my hand on my heart, I hold my breath as he pauses. "We found the man who died on the river, trapped face-down in some logs."

I was fucking right.

Two firefighters, including my husband (Swift Water rescue), and a police officer were on the trip and pulled this man out of the river, got him to the ranger's station, and then home to his family on Father's Day.

My dream flashes repeatedly in my head. I watch it in real time as he recounts the story and the role he and his team played that day.

My mind spins with the visions and the messages that come in next:

You did see it. You did dream it. You're not crazy. That literally happened.

The river called to you. You may not have gotten it 100% correct;

Your husband didn't die, but what you will learn later,

is that it was the beginning of the death of your relationship.

Of course, my body rejects the last message. Yet I know. I move into the guest room before he gets home.

We went an entire year without triggering each other before this experience, but it was bound to happen, and apparently, it needed to happen over the Solstice portal. And I needed to be alone for it. I'm proud of our ability to communicate and work through the misalignments. And now I understand the mask he was wearing, and this was the first crack.

I forgive him and I stay, because I believe him when he says he left because of his own trauma around his first marriage.

We're human, and the greatest and most powerful teaching that gets me through this whole ordeal was the fact that we, as humans, can hold duality.

I love you with everything I am. And. *You dropped me.*

It reminds me I'm whole, all by myself. I get myself through this ordeal without the help of my significant other. I don't need him. I choose to have him in my life in this role we agreed on. It leads to further communication around what unconditional love, relationships, and boundaries look like and what I want and need from a business partner versus an intimate partner.

The clarity from our experience and communication takes us into a deeper yes from both sides to continue with an intimate relationship at this time.

Does forgiving him and staying in this relationship serve me?

Three years later:

As I recapitulate this experience, I see the patterns of being dropped repeatedly, and not just by this now ex-husband.

I abandoned myself more in this life than any other human.
I see the choice in my partners to choose others over beloveds.

Loyalty isn't a thing in most people's world, leaving most relationships transactional.

I gave my love the shape of understanding.
I handed him the benefit of the doubt, dressed in sacred empathy.

And still, I bled alone.
I healed alone.
I resurrected alone.

What happens when the healer is left bleeding?
She becomes her own resurrection.

✟ℍℰ 𝕸ℰ𝔻𝕀ℭ𝕀ℕℰ

THE MOTHER WOUND AND THE MIRROR

There's a specific kind of betrayal that happens when a woman becomes the healer, the mother, and the container for a man's unprocessed pain. She doesn't just love him, she *understands* him, empathizes with him, forgives what hasn't even been named.

This is called **over-functioning.**
It's also a **sacred distortion** of the feminine.
We're taught that to be loved, **we must stay.**
We're taught that to be spiritual, we must forgive.

And we're told that understanding someone's pain means absorbing the consequences of it.

But the truth is this: Empathy is not consent.

Compassion isn't a contract to keep bleeding for someone else's wound.

And forgiveness doesn't mean returning to the fire that burned you.

This is where the *Mirror Clause* comes in.

The Mirror Clause: "I will reflect your pain, but I won't carry it for you."

You're not his mother. You're not his therapist.
You're not his place to run from intimacy and call it trauma.
You can hold space for his story without giving up your own safety, body, or becoming.

You can say:

"I see you. I believe your pain is real. And I'm not the one who must pay for it."

"I no longer shrink the truth of what I lived through
for the comfort of those who couldn't hold it."

PRACTICE: THE MIRROR CLAUSE

- Light a candle. Place a mirror before you.
- Speak aloud the roles you've played to try and keep love: mother, healer, forgiver, saint.
- Now say: "I release myself from contracts that required my self-abandonment."
- Hold your gaze in the mirror and declare: "I can love and still leave. I can forgive and still say no."
- Breathe. Reclaim.

JOURNAL PROMPT:

Where have I mistaken compassion for obligation?
Who have I mothered in place of being met?

Be gentle with yourself as you traverse these deep, subconscious layers of self-abandonment and bring awareness into your being.

Re-introduce yourself to these feral aspects within that need love and tenderness so they can start to remember that it's safe to be with you, and no longer need to hide.

TO MY INNER CHILD:

I am so proud of you, my love.
Thank you for having the courage and the will to work through the repair with me, to bring our multidimensional self back into wholeness.

Your bravery is acknowledged and your light revered in our internal world. You will never again be left behind as we traverse this new timeline on Earth. I will always have your hand in mine and your heart tucked deep inside, safe and protected, always.

TO MY BRAVE READER:

Thank you for witnessing my journey and allowing your inner child to witness what it looks like to be acknowledged. I understand it's scary and dysregulating. I'm here if you need assistance in reconnecting with your inner child and starting this work into wholeness. You can find my contact information at the back, in the "About the Author" page.

Solar hugs and many blessings on your journey.

I NO LONGER SHRINK THE TRUTH OF WHAT I LIVED THROUGH
FOR THE COMFORT OF THOSE WHO COULDN'T HOLD IT.

~ ANGEL GOLD

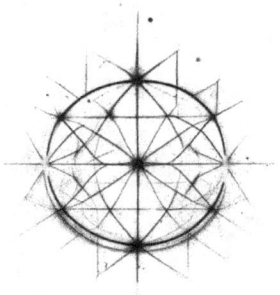

Chapter 9

PLEA OF THE WARRIORESS TO RETURN TO THE SACRED HEART

How to Turn Self-Sabotage into Self-Mastery

Grace Solaris

𝕸𝖞 𝕾𝖙𝖔𝖗𝖞

As I stood gazing into the endless tapestry of the starry night, I wondered:

Which one is it?

Could it be that one, so bright and twinkling?

The yearning was piercing through my heart, and it would not let go until I found the answer. A seeking and calling that would become louder and louder. I knew for sure, I wasn't of this crude and cold world. Deep within my heart, I knew I came here to make a difference.

My heart trembled as I felt the sword of my father's raging voice cutting through the air. The Earth was shivering, as was every cell in my body. Terror pulsated through my skin, and my heart throbbed in my throat as I ran down the hallway. I made it just in time and was able to turn the lock before his hand could grab me. Had I not made it, the outcome would have been a furious spanking!

None of it made sense.

What had I done? What was it in me that ignited the anger in his heart?

I had become his favorite prey and target to release the unresolved anger of his inner child.

This was a scene playing itself out repeatedly throughout my childhood. I felt unsafe, guilty, and shameful. I would rather hide from the world, and so I dimmed my light, and at times, I hid in the closet for hours, crying my heart out.

I became an outcast, but the child within didn't understand, because in my heart, I knew I was here for love —to shine light and love into the world.

My mother was absent in her depression. I sensed she was entrapped, hiding inside a void of hopelessness. I sensed a wall of protection keeping me from reaching into her heart. No hope. I was on my own. So, I decided I had to take things into my own hands.

The warrioress within came to my rescue, but my inner child was broken and tormented by the echo of the roaring thunder of my dad's voice.

"How could you, you naughty girl? I'm going to teach you a lesson." As a teen, an ever-returning thought repeated itself inside my mind:

If I can't do that, I might as well pack my suitcase and leave the planet.

Deep within my heart, I knew I came to heal the world and restore harmony. But I also knew what I was called to do wouldn't happen overnight. My heart was impatient.

The yearning to get on with my mission to bring love and healing was like an arrow piercing deeper and deeper into my heart.

Do not forget, keep going; your time will come.

I became a rebel; I wasn't made to obey. I questioned everything because I couldn't ignore the inner knowing of my heart. I stood up against authority.

Who the fuck are you to tell me what's right and wrong?

Who are you to judge me and belittle me?

So, I set forth my journey to make a change because I knew within my heart that something wasn't right. But I was tortured by the derogatory loop of thoughts of not being good enough and that something was wrong with me. I started building up walls of protection around me.

The voice of my heart turned increasingly silent.

I became trapped inside my mind.

I knew I had to watch my tongue, but the inner warrioress wouldn't give in.

"You're going to do as I say." A deep-seated rage escaped my dad's ice-blue eyes, causing my body to shiver, and yet I insisted, "No, I'm not." He desperately searched for something to grab and suddenly aimed at me with a coat hanger. His face had morphed into a demon, hardly recognizable. I flinched in a split second and avoided the hit.

The warrioress was not going to allow his physical punishments to continue.

She quickly found balance and took a step towards him. "Don't you dare." The sacred rage of the warrioress caused him to freeze. "No more," she roared.

And yet I was paying less and less attention to the voice of my inner child. She felt alone and defeated. I disconnected from the earth, my body, and my heart to avoid the grief piling up inside me.

I dimmed my light to avoid the broken child in me from being seen. However, the warrioress was not going to submit.

She wasn't made to be ruled by someone, but to reign from her heart. The voice of my divine feminine, the inner warrioress was fierce and impossible to silence.

You think you are going to break me by hitting and scaring me. With years of suppression, my dignity and confidence shrank.

Should I just give in?

No way!

She left me no choice but to keep fighting for my freedom and love.

I got up and wiped the tears away, my jaw clenching as I found the strength yet again. She was determined. Nevertheless, my inner child suffered the loss of her innocence at the striking hand of my dad. My heart quivered in my mother's silence and inability to defend me, leaving no space for hope.

The emotional and physical abuse became fuel to my search for God, and so the journey began.

I dove into every religion, belief system, and philosophy I could lay my hands on to find a sense of belonging, from the ancient religions of India to the native mythology and tales of the stars. I signed up for a mystery school, a two-year training, and initiation into the wisdom of ancient Lemuria and Atlantis. My awakening was accelerating; however, again, I witnessed how patriarchal dominance gave birth to submission and fake worship.

I saw how so many gave their power away to external 'father figures' and abandoned their inner knowing.

One and a half years into the training, my higher self suddenly stepped in and said:

No more.

This has no value to you.

You are giving your power away. You are not being true to your heart.

I realized what I was taught was just a mind concept, but what my heart was yearning for was a deep, heartfelt, embodied experience through surrendering to my inner truth. Only by being true to my heart could I be authentic and love myself. So, I dropped out. I was guided to burn the entire material of one and a half years of training. I burnt every single paper in my stove, one by one, stripping me to the core like an onion, until there was nothing left but an excruciating black void.

This sparked off my dark night of the soul.

I found myself in a void of not knowing. I felt vulnerable and naked to the core. I felt like a failure. This lasted for months, until one day when I felt ready to reconnect with God and open my heart unreservedly. I fell on my knees begging God to respond to my longing for home.

"Dear God, I am here before you naked to the core. All I want is to serve you and make a difference in the world." My heart cried out:

"How can I serve you?"

An immense wave of love washed over me, permeating every cell of my body and restoring my dignity as I was held in the embrace of God.

I was ready to embark on the journey to unite with the beloved within. I was free of the need for external validation. The stripping of the teaching and beliefs also initiated a stripping of my incarnational story and the identity that played it out to perfection.

I fell apart piece by piece until, one night, the last piece —the foundation of the jigsaw—broke apart. I laughed out loud as the realization and remembrance of who I AM came into my awareness, exploding from every cell.

Love is who and what I AM, no more, no less.

All veils lifted in an instant; as I understood, I created it all. I felt uplifted, empowered, and infinite joy filled my entire being as my wings of freedom unfurled. The goddess in me rose in her true glory.

Suddenly, it became clear how the patriarchal dominion and agenda, repressing the divine feminine aspect throughout the ages, had played itself out in my personal story.

The goddess in me had a different agenda, refusing to submit to the distortions of patriarchal superiority.

She knew the importance of balancing heart and mind and that this is the key to divine equilibrium and union with God. Through the balancing of the divine feminine and masculine aspects within, the inner beloved is birthed.

The divine feminine and masculine have been fighting an endless battle, creating extreme distortion, power plays, rivalry, and suffering within all humans, and between genders, cultures, and nations, keeping us divided from God.

I realized that all the suffering I went through was a preparation for fulfilling my mission as a midwife, helping others unite with God within and live a life of joy.

From there, the eternal love affair with the beloved within began, as my inner divine feminine and masculine united and balance was restored. I learned how to give up control and surrender to the graceful unfolding of life under the heart-aligned leadership of the divine feminine.

I learned that life is effortless and full of grace when we let go and trust in the flow of life. I realized that the more I let go and surrendered to the guidance of the divine feminine force in me, the more life became a dance.

All you need is to be fully grounded in the heart of the present moment— this is the only place where you're aligned and attuned to God. When you get out of your mind into your heart, you're bypassing the interference of ego, which is obsessed with keeping control in its aim to protect you from the suffering of the past.

By being entrapped in the past and in your mind, you're attracting what you're trying to avoid and projecting it into the future. You're living a life in avoidance of what you fear the most.

The nature of the mind is limited by linear thinking and ruled by masculine attributes. It is action-oriented and led by logic and reason, whereas the divine feminine is founded in feeling, intuition, and surrender.

Both need to be given space to fulfill their purpose.

However, the divine feminine is the natural principle aligning you with the cosmic flow, which nurtures and keeps you attuned to the truth. She's the seed of all life and the leading principle of creation.

The sacred purpose of the divine masculine is to guard and implement what she intuits, senses, and receives through deep surrender to God.

Everything in the universe is frequency attracting the corresponding reality.

Every thought, feeling, and act holds a frequency attracting the corresponding external response and manifestation into the physical world. This is the key principle to understanding why situations and specific patterns keep repeating themselves, despite your trying to avoid them. By dwelling in your mind, you're limited by experiences of the past.

To live a life of fulfillment, joy, and abundance, you need to be in a vibrational match with your heart's desire. You need to embody it, smelling, tasting, and feeling it in every cell of your body, as if you already have it. By vibrating it, you're giving it life. It takes conscious intent and deep surrender to allow things to manifest in whatever way serves your highest good.

Surrendering to the inner knowing and intelligence of your heart is living under the guidance and leadership of your divine feminine aspect. It's allowing life to live itself through you without the mind interrupting the natural flow.

So, my love, dare to move beyond fear into the unknown, the unfamiliar, the untried, the outrageous, the juicy stuff making your heart sing with joy, even when your ego screams, "Get me out of here."

It's time to trust your wings.

It's time to soar higher beyond the comfort zone of the known.

This isn't the time for playing it safe; it won't get you where you long to be. It's a time of exploration and discovery of unknown paths that no one ever made before you. There are no maps or signs other than following your intuition and inner guidance.

There is no way you are going to figure out where and what to do next.

Plant seeds of intent with your heart here and there and see where energy is flowing and where things are growing. This is where you'll find doors appearing, showing you your divine purpose and the steps needed to get there.

It's the doorway to the greatest love story in your life, a safe passageway to home.

The inner beloved will walk beside you, guard you, and guide you. You don't need to know how, when, or what.

Only ego wants to know. And ego wants it complicated.

The path will show itself as you're moving forward with unwavering trust in your heart's inner knowing. All it takes is your uncompromising "yes." You were made to create miracles, make the impossible possible, transcend all limitations, and live an untamed life of passion.

You came here to make a difference and to lead from your heart.

The Medicine

Allow me to introduce you to this healing space, where you can go at any time to receive healing and comfort.

It's the womb of the cosmic mother where you can bring all the lost and fragmented parts of you into wholeness. It's the place where you can receive healing, bring home your inner child, and restore the balance between your divine feminine and masculine. It's a place where you can do forgiveness work and release deep trauma.

It's a place of rebirth, resurrection, and sacred union. Below is a brief example of a guided meditation on how to utilize this cave.

So, my love, let me take you by the hand and lead you into this healing space.

First, I'm asking you to take a moment to relax and let go of all control in your body. Still your mind; allow your thoughts to drift by like clouds in the sky and come into the sanctum of your heart.

Now imagine yourself growing solid roots out of your feet down to the center of the Earth, keep going until you cannot get further, and then anchor deep into the core of Mother Earth.

Start breathing in through your nose, deep into the belly, and as you exhale, let go of all the tension in your body.

Allow yourself to be. You can be safe here.

You do not need to perform or pretend to be someone different than who you are.

Take a few minutes to breathe deeply into your heart, and as you release your breath, let all tension leave your body and empty your mind.

Allow yourself to sink into stillness.

Now imagine yourself entering a cave made of pure rose quartz.

The light is soft and warm, and in the middle of the cave, you see a circle of women dressed in long, crystalline, sparkling robes of light holding hands.

You are urged to step into the middle of the circle.

Now take a few moments to greet each of these beautiful, radiant beings, who are smiling at you with such warmth.

You recognize many of the faces and feel overwhelmed by the love emanating from each of them. Each carries a gift of love, a divine virtue of the divine feminine, which is for your healing. One or two might even have a message for you, so listen carefully with your heart.

When you've finished connecting with each of the goddesses, you're ready to call on all aspects of your inner child that have been left in the dark, abandoned, and separated from you. It is time to bring them home. Call from your heart to each of these aspects to come forth and tell them it's time for them to return home and to become whole again.

Now, wait and allow for each of them to show up in their divine timing.

One may be reluctant, another may be scared, and another may be timid.

State to your beloved inner child:

I am here with an open heart and open arms to offer you my love. Know that you are safe, that there's nothing to fear. I'm here for you, so please come closer and let me hold you. Let the tears of feeling unworthy and unlovable leave your heart, know that you matter to me and the world. I see you, beloved child, I see the gift of love in your heart. I love you exactly as you are. Come into my embrace and know you're safe now.

I'm here for you from this moment onwards.

I ask you to please forgive me and trust me. You shall never be abandoned again, never forgotten or forsaken.

I'm committed to guarding you and always love you.

Let go of the shame and guilt, the condemnation and judgment, that have weighed on your heart.

Let go of the burden on your shoulders that you have carried for others. You were meant to shine, beloved child. Remember who you are.

No more silencing, no more dimming your light. You are now free to be who you came to be. Free to speak your heart and express your truth.

You are loved and always one with me. Let's go out and play. I want to see the world of wonders through your eyes.

We are a team now, unbreakable, and victorious.

I am a spiritual leader, teacher, mentor, psychic, and multi-dimensional healer. I'm the voice of the divine feminine and embodiment of divine grace, here to lead you back into wholeness to enable you to live your highest soul potential and wildest dreams.

It's my greatest passion to assist you in discovering your unique gifts and talents and guide you home to your natural state of divine joy. To assist you in removing everything that prevents you from living your fullest potential, so you can step into divine leadership in service to God.

I have 14 years of experience empowering my soul tribe to greater joy, passion, and soul fulfillment on all levels of their life, to greater health and wealth. My gift is to tap into and pinpoint where you are sabotaging and withholding love from yourself. I've assisted thousands in healing from deep trauma, including sexual abuse, addictions, and self-destructive behaviors, to catalyze radical and rapid quantum shifts in their lives. I help identify where you're giving your power away and refrain from making healthy choices, and why.

I work on multiple levels to clear wounds from this and previous lifetimes and to facilitate groundbreaking results by clearing old vows, agreements, and mindsets holding you back from stepping into your full potential. I'm here to guide you through the dark night of the soul to reclaim your true might and light.

I'm available for one-on-one sessions, mentorship programs, and facilitate group activations and retreats.

Connect with Grace:

Website: https://www.graceelohim.com

Email: info@graceelohim.com

Facebook: https://www.facebook.com/grace66solaris/

Visit my Soundcloud for free guided meditations:
https://soundcloud.com/grace-solaris

YouTube: https://www.youtube.com/@graceelohim1/featured

OH, YES SAID LOVE. YOU CAN TRY TO RUN AWAY FROM ME,
BUT I WILL WAIT IN YOUR SACRED HEART LIKE A PATIENT LOVER
UNTIL YOU RETURN TO ME. I WILL NEVER GIVE UP ON YOU.
I AM WHO YOU TRULY ARE.

~ GRACE SOLARIS

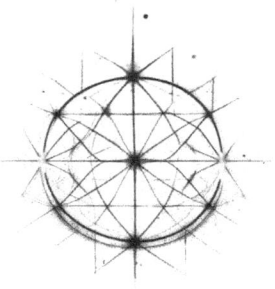

Chapter 10

SUCCESS WITH SHADOWS

Awakening The Nervous System To Leadership
Spencer Macdonald

𝕸y 𝕾t⊕ry

I told myself I broke the cycle.

For a boy who was abandoned, abused, and tossed into the foster system
at age three, this felt like triumph.

By the time I was 21, I thought I had life figured out. Money came
easy, faster than I ever imagined when I was a kid shuffling between foster
residences and group homes. I drove the car I wanted, ate at restaurants I
never thought I'd afford, and dated women I once considered far beyond
my reach. I told myself I was proud.

Beneath the gloss of early success lived a hunger I couldn't satisfy.
Alcohol entered my bloodstream at 14 and quickly became a daily dance.

By 15, cannabis was my daily ritual, smoke clouds softening the sharp
edges of my mind and nervous system. Psychedelics and stimulants entered
on weekends or during concerts—special occasions I justified as "living

young." I always reached for something outside myself to prove I was enough, to soothe the raw ache that still lived in my cells.

On the surface, I looked like a young man in control. Inside, I was a boy who was never taught how to sit with himself.

When I booked my trip to the largest spa in Canada, I wasn't looking for transformation. I looked for an escape. The itinerary rested on the hotel bed, listing spa appointments: a regular massage, a couple's session, and one more, a mysterious treatment I half-heartedly asked about in an email.

At the time, I was angry that they signed me up without my consent. "Probably overpriced," I muttered. But massages were one of my favorite indulgences as a high-performance athlete. My body was familiar with deep tissue work, the kind that forced sore muscles to release after long hockey seasons. Something about the phrase *light touch* caught my eye. Gentle, easy, maybe even forgettable.

I woke the next morning to my usual routine: quick rip of the bong before breakfast, an attempt at food to ground the high, and a lazy stroll to the spa for my 11:00 a.m. appointment. I didn't think much about it. Just another hour of touch, another way to treat myself.

That's when Angel greeted me.

A DIFFERENT KIND OF HEALING

The room was dim, ambient space music played, and a massage table waited.

"Have you ever done anything like this before?" she asked, her voice calm, steady.

"Sorta." I shrugged. "Played hockey my whole life, so I've had a lot of work done to keep my body flexible."

She smiled gently, but her words weren't about muscles. She spoke of energy, of chakras, of holding and releasing—words I only vaguely heard in the occasional yoga class for goaltenders. This is when I became aware of how high I actually was. My head hummed as she explained how the practice used energetics.

My inner skeptic arrived: *What the fuck did I sign up for?*

But another part of me—the part that learned to survive by adapting, by listening to those more educated than me—awakened, and there I was in student mode. If I was going to pay for this, I'd give it a chance.

I lay on the table, eyes covered, body open to whatever this "light touch" might be.

Her hands hovered over my back, not pressing, not kneading, but moving energy I couldn't see. At first, it was subtle. Almost nothing. Then—something shifted.

It was as if her hands reached inside me without touching. Wherever she focused, I felt heat, pulsing pressure, and maybe even a sense of collapse. Old pain stirred—memories stored in my muscles, tightness I didn't even realize I carried.

Awareness brought discomfort, but also release.

My body wanted to let go, but letting go was harder than holding on.

It was *not* painless.

When she finished my back, I thought the session was almost over. I had no idea the true journey hadn't even begun.

THE BREAKTHROUGH

I rolled onto my back. Her hand landed on my chest and stomach. Instantly, everything changed.

My breath fractured into rapid, shallow gasps; I hyperventilated without warning. Sweat poured from every part, heat flooding my skin. My covered eyes filled with a brightness that pierced through the fabric. Time slowed, stretched, collapsed.

And then I was gone.

I wasn't in the spa anymore. I wasn't a 21-year-old athlete lying on a table. I watched my life unfold in a way that was orchestrated and already completed. I was shown that I chose those youthful years of hardship and confusion to help myself have a deeper understanding of struggle so I could have more patience and relate more easily later in life.

My biological mother appeared, not in flesh but in my vision.

Memories unfolded without sound, yet the messages were crystal clear. I saw the years I was shuffled through foster homes, the grief of being both supported and abandoned, the unbearable loneliness of waiting for someone to claim me, and no one staying long enough.

Lua emerged—the woman I later called Mom.

A complicated relationship that brought both love and structure and shame in later life. I saw Meaghan, my oldest sister, her face carried through photos, the echoes of our shared pain and our shared agreements.

For 14 years, I lived inside a system that broke more than it healed. And for the first time, I understood not only what happened, but why my body and soul chose to endure it.

The drugs made sense now. They weren't just rebellion, they were self-medication, crude attempts to still a nervous system on fire since childhood.

A VISION STRONGER THAN ANY HIGH

I took seven grams of mushrooms before. I dropped MDMA and chased euphoric highs that blurred into empty crashes. None of it compared to this.

This was clarity—hallucinations sharper than any drug could produce.

Love stronger than any chemical could mimic.

It wasn't an escape; it was an arrival.

I didn't run from my pain. I faced it, enveloped in a love I never knew, held by something greater than myself.

When the visions subsided, when my breath slowed and my body cooled, I knew something fundamental had changed.

The success I built, the money, the women, the bravado, suddenly felt flimsy. My identity as the tough, self-made foster kid who "made it" shattered in an instant.

And yet, I wasn't destroyed. I was remade.

For the first time, I understood leadership was not about control or performance. It was about surrender, about courage to feel, about facing the shadows that shape us and loving their gifts, instead of numbing them.

That session wasn't the end of my healing. It was the beginning. The doorway cracked open by Angel's hand on my chest demanded I walk through, again and again.

I had to learn new ways of regulating my body without substances. I had to look at the parts of me that still clung to validation. I had to face the boy inside me who only wanted to be chosen—and teach him I would choose him now.

The journey has not been easy.

But every leader worth following is first forged in fire.

My fire came in the form of abandonment, addiction,

and a light touch that shattered me open.

~ Spencer

*

Hmm, he's something special, I note as I walk down the crystal-lined hallway, off to my next massage appointment. My hands start buzzing as I reach for my client list. I call for my person, and he stands up. *Huh? Weird, he already had a massage today.*

We enter my room; "How exciting, your first Reiki treatment!" I offered as I energetically scanned him, explaining what was about to happen.

He's face down. I make big, swooping motions up and down his spine, across his hips, drawing the energy up to his head, drawing circles with my nails through his hair as the crown energy releases into the air.

His body softens, big exhales as I repeat the process over and over, slowly removing his energetic armor.

He drops in as my hands heat his lower back, circling, massaging his hips, calling in the element of fire. *His trauma is deep.* My brows furrow. *This one's powerful.* I grow my roots and expand wider. His body responds to my deep roots. His breathing shifts deeper as I feel his *yes* sink into his bones.

His armor falls off. It's go time.

I waste no time flipping him over, knowing the window is fleeting and timing is everything. Calling in light codes, ancestors, and guides, opening the aperture of his chest with my left, circling over and over as my right hand slides and lands on his solar plexus. The energy inside his body is on high alert and looking for an escape route. Shaking, he's in deep breathwork. I anchor and hold as he navigates his nervous system and what's being unearthed from the archival depths.

Yes? I ask energetically. His body drops into dead stillness; his breath becomes faint. *He's diving, go now.* I don't hesitate and slide my hand down to his lower abs with the precision of a surgeon, spreading wildfire with my fingers across his belly.

His stomach responds, convulsing as I slowly, ever so softly, surgically express his wound. Acute awareness drops around us; the air thickens as the energetic shift deepens. Deep breathing and sweating; he's at his edge. I hold a little longer while he rides the wave, hunting for the deep subconscious space in need of unlocking.

Tap, tap, tap, my laser fingers zero in on his heart. "Let it go," I whisper. *Tap, tap, tap.* "You don't need to carry this any longer." Small circles of fire on his lower stomach; *tap, tap, tap* on his heart.

He finds the key and turns it. Erupting emotions spill out through sweat, snot, and tears as I pull his arm up and out to the side, pulling the energy from his belly up his chest and out his hand over and over. I move to the other side; lifetimes of residual trauma stream from his heart as the re-attachment of his wings begins.

Shhhh. I lay my hands on his chest, my third eye just above his, beaming love into his heart, pulling him into the Earth. The temple of the mother flashes in my awareness. I hold space as his DNA restructures itself.

Stillness sets in. I sit at his head, one hand on his heart, one on his third eye, connecting us like a constellation in the sky, tears slowly drip down the side of his face as I softly run my hands across his forehead, and through his hair, "How you doin'?" I softly check in as my fingers turn circles on his temples.

~ Angel

The Medicine

What I carried from that room, dripping in sweat and shaking in awe, was more than a personal revelation. It was leadership medicine.

Leaders are not those who hide their wounds. Leaders are those who dare to walk through them, to feel them, to allow their pain to become wisdom.

I always thought leadership meant being the strongest, the most successful, the one no one could knock down. But the truth revealed itself in that session: Leadership is about becoming radically honest. It's about allowing vulnerability to transform into vision.

My nervous system wrote the script of my life since I was three years old. Trauma made me reactive, defensive, and addicted to control. But in that moment of surrender, I understood that healing my nervous system was the key to becoming the kind of leader who could truly and deeply hold space for others.

Not a leader who dominates, but a leader who understands. Not a leader who performs, but a leader who embodies.

I came to that session a boy disguised as a man. I left knowing the path to becoming a true man—a true leader—would not be built on money, women, or drugs. It would be built on healing, courage, and on the discipline to sit in the fire without numbing out.

Leadership starts by awakening your nervous system—not numbing it.

Not ignoring it. Awakening it.

Because the leader who can breathe through his own shadows is the one who can stand steady when the people around him are falling apart.

You don't need a mystical session to begin. You need a practice, a way to remind your body that it's safe to stay, feel, and respond.

THE NERVOUS SYSTEM LEADERSHIP PRACTICE

Step 1: Root in the Body
Stand with your feet hip-width apart, close your eyes. Feel the floor beneath you. Spread your toes and imagine roots pressing into the ground. This is your anchor. You are not separate from the Earth—its strengths are your strengths.

Step 2: Breathe With Power
Inhale slowly through your nose for a count of four. Hold for a count of two. Exhale through your mouth for a count of six. Repeat five times. Longer exhales tell your nervous system: *You are safe.*

Step 3: Scan the Shadows
Notice where tension hides—in your jaw, chest, or gut. Instead of pushing it away, place a hand there and say quietly: *I see you. I can hold this. I allow this. I soften into this.* Awareness melts armor.

Step 4: Open the Channel
Notice the subtle space between inhale and exhale, sensation and silence. This is the portal of presence. Rest your awareness here, letting masculine and feminine currents meet.

Step 5: Choose from Options
Ask yourself: *What does this moment need from me?* Realizing the options

that are available, not from fear or habit, but from presence. Sometimes the answer is action. Sometimes it's stillness. Both can be strengths.

When you practice this, you train your body to lead.

You learn that leadership is not domination; it's regulation.

It's not about being untouchable; it's about being unshakable.

That is the invitation I leave with you: don't numb, don't run.

Awaken. Lead from your nervous system outward.

That one hour with Angel changed the trajectory of my life.

It showed me that no substance, success, or external validation could ever give me what I sought.

What I sought was myself.

And in that room, for the first time, I saw him.

Spencer MacDonald's path to leadership began not in boardrooms or classrooms, but in the fire of lived experience. Abandoned at three years old and raised inside the Canadian foster care system, Spencer learned early how to adapt, endure, and survive. By his early 20s, he built the image of success—athlete, entrepreneur, provider—but beneath the surface lived a nervous system still carrying the raw ache of abandonment, addiction, and unprocessed trauma.

Everything shifted the day he stepped into a healing room and experienced a light-touch energy session that cracked him open. What began as skepticism became surrender, and in that surrender, Spencer discovered the deeper meaning of resilience: not the ability to hold it all together, but the courage to let go.

Spencer went on to train with Angel Gold as a Usui Reiki Practitioner Level 2, refining his natural sensitivity into a disciplined, energetic practice. His initiation into the subtle realms gave him a new compass for leadership, one rooted not in dominance, but in presence.

In 2024, he entered a profound apprenticeship with Angel Gold inside *Nina Songo: Fire Heart Mystery School,* where he continues to deepen his study of Toltec wisdom, Celtic shamanic practice, and the embodiment of what it means to lead from the nervous system outward.

Today, Spencer blends lived experience, athletic discipline, and energetic medicine into a unique leadership framework. He works with humans to awaken the wisdom hidden inside their shadows, guiding them to embody their masculine and feminine aspects within.

His message is simple but radical: True leadership isn't about avoiding the fire, but about standing inside it with courage, humility, and heart.

Connect with Spencer:

Website: https://spencermacdonald.com

Instagram: https://www.instagram.com/spencermacd/

THE JOURNEY HAS NOT BEEN EASY.
BUT EVERY LEADER WORTH FOLLOWING HAS BEEN FORGED IN FIRE.

~ SPENCER MACDONALD

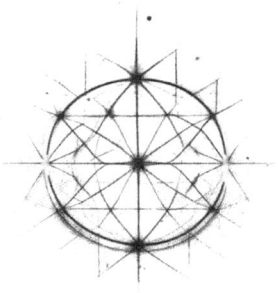

Chapter 11

FROM FLIGHT TO FIGHT

Transmuting Trauma into Strength

Kristina Skye, BSc, C.H.N.C.

My Story

"Say it!" he screamed.

"Say it and I'll let you get up. Tell me that you do not believe in God!"

I could feel the weight of his hands pressing down onto my shoulders as he straddled my small frame.

"No," I whispered. "I can't say that."

The pressure in my head grew as I fought to hold back tears. His impatience was building; the vein bulged above his left temple as his face deepened to crimson. We had been locked in this standoff for what felt like an eternity. I had struggled at first, but the competitive weightlifter was winning. My struggle was futile.

He took a deep breath and tried to regain some composure. His face softened as his grip on my arms loosened.

"Why do you believe in God?" he asked. "How can you believe in God? Give me proof – evidence."

"How can you not?" I replied. In my 21-year-old mind, I couldn't believe that anyone could truly be an atheist. Surely not the man that I'd chosen to commit myself to.

"There's no scientific evidence," he said. "If you can give me scientific evidence, then you can believe in God."

My body went limp. I closed my eyes. My heart pounded in my ears as I retreated into my own thoughts. My thoughts were scattered, going in a million different directions.

How can someone else tell me what to think?

That's not okay. Why do I have to justify my beliefs?

Please let the baby wake up. Then surely, he will let me go get the baby.

How can I make this stop?

"Sometimes you don't need scientific evidence to believe something," I finally whispered, my heart sinking.

He disagreed. My eyes burned. I couldn't hold back the tears anymore— they slid silently down the sides of my face. Silence permeated the room as he steadily maintained his position of power over me, on all levels – physically, emotionally, and even spiritually.

I looked away in submission. Defeated, I couldn't meet his gaze.

A cry broke the silence. The baby was awake.

I looked expectantly back at my husband. "Just say it," he demanded one more time. "Tell me you don't believe in God, then we can get the baby."

I looked away. It was in that moment that I chose to give my power away.

"Fine," I whispered, so low that maybe—just maybe—God wouldn't hear.

"I don't believe in God."

I was never the athletic girl.

Never the sporty girl.

I was the smart girl.

The academic.

As a child, I chose quiet activities. I found solace in books—that was my safe space, my time to recharge. I was usually smaller than most girls my age and never considered myself physically strong. As the daughter of an ex-marine, I didn't need to be strong. Boys were supposed to be strong. Girls were supposed to be smart. That was the story I told myself for over forty years. It seemed true in my childhood home, and that narrative continued when I married a competitive weightlifter.

Years later, that marriage fell apart, and I was left on my own – a single mother of four. I returned to school and earned a Bachelor of Health Science degree. *Surely that'll solve all my problems—get smarter.* Not surprisingly, it didn't.

I watched as my parents' health deteriorated and my father, the strongest man I ever knew, fell and eventually died from complications of a hip fracture.

After his fall, I had to take a good, hard look at myself. *What happened to me over the years?* Despite everything I did, I struggled to achieve balance. *Do I want to end up like my parents?* I gained a significant amount of weight and barely recognized myself anymore.

In the spring of 2019, I joined a gym. I had joined gyms before – paid membership fees for years – but seldom, if ever, went.

This time, **I vowed,** *would be different.*

At first, this was a journey of health. I committed to going three times a week. I did for the first while, but then life got in the way, as it always does. I started nutrition school and dropped to twice a week. COVID arrived and gave me an excellent excuse to abandon my commitment to my body for a year and a half, even though I saw the results of more energy and changes in my body.

In the spring of 2021, COVID restrictions were lifted, and I went back to the gym. This time, I committed to five days a week. When I went before, my three-day commitment was easy to let slide. "Oh, I'm tired, I'll just go tomorrow," or "I want to meet a friend," or any other excuse as a reason to turn around. *There's always tomorrow.*

The transformation started happening when I decided to go every day. It became a routine; it was just what I did after work. I didn't have to think about it; I just went. I started looking forward to going to the gym,

I consistently felt better after each workout, and I enjoyed the extra energy I never had before.

My mindset shifted again, and I realized that hour in the gym could be mine.

It became self-care. In my busy life, it was the one moment a day I had completely to myself. My thoughts were my own, and I was able to leave work and home behind. It became a meditative practice, and the most important part of my day.

Slowly, my body started to change once again. I developed strength I didn't know I could. At almost 50 years old, I'm as strong as any of the younger girls in that gym. I can see muscle definition for the first time in my life. The physical strength I've gained has helped me to gain balance. I'm now stronger, not only physically but mentally and emotionally. But I still can't do a cartwheel!

Physical strength has given me the ability to reclaim and efficiently manage the parts of myself I lost.

The Medicine

Unless you've been living under a rock, you've probably heard of the fight or flight response. This is the body's response to a threat, either perceived or real. It's a stress response. It's an important mechanism when stress is short-lived, but becomes problematic during times of chronic stress. When this response is triggered, your hormone balance is thrown off, and your adrenal glands start to overproduce cortisol and adrenaline. Short-term, this is great.

For our ancestors, it helped them get away from that tiger chasing them or to fight off invading predators. Unfortunately, our bodies don't recognize the difference between stress caused by these types of isolated incidents and the modern stresses we encounter every day. Trauma leads to stress.

Often, the stress induced by trauma doesn't just go away when the incident is over. Just as we hold onto the trauma, our body continues to function as if under stress. The results of this on the body over time lead to dysfunction, dysregulation, and disease. Just look around.

Our modern population is plagued by an epidemic of obesity, diabetes, anxiety, depression, heart disease, hypertension, and even cancers. What do all these things have in common? They can all be linked to high levels of cortisol. Why does the stress caused by trauma lead to sustained levels of cortisol in the long term? Because trauma changes how we think. It changes how we perceive the world. It teaches us to live in a world of fear where we don't ever feel completely safe. We learn not to let our guard down. And the body responds accordingly.

If we hope to change this response, we need to first deal with the trauma. Trauma is never two-dimensional. It's always multi-faceted, and as such, you need to take a multi-faceted approach to deal with past trauma. Unless you address the trifecta of mind, body, and spirit, you'll never resolve the trauma.

In order to make a change,

you must first decide that you're going to make a change.

While it's not easy, it can be done.

The first step is to be honest with yourself. Then, ask yourself the following questions:

- What is it that needs to change?

- Why do you need to make a change?

- What would it look like if you made the change?

- Who will this change affect in your world?

- When will you start to implement these changes? Are you ready to take action and take back your power?

I would argue that "why" is the most important question of all. Without this answer, the rest is moot.

Only when you can self-reflect and answer these questions honestly will you even be able to consider change.

Are you ready to step into your authenticity and accept yourself as you truly are?

This is the space where transformation can begin.

The thing about addressing trauma is that there are just as many ways to address the trauma as there are people in this world. The answer will be unique to each individual. The way you decide to approach this is going to be different than the way I have decided to approach it. We all experience trauma at some point in our lives.

None of us leaves this planet unscathed.

I encourage you to try many different things to find the thing or the combination of things that'll work for you. There's counseling, and counseling absolutely helps, but even with counseling, unless you're ready to do the work, its effectiveness will be limited. I'm a strong advocate for counseling, and I do believe that for many, it can and should be part of their approach to healing trauma. Just know that it's not a magic pill.

There are no magic pills.

The medicine is in the work you choose to do.

Its effectiveness will match the energy that you put in.

If you want extra-strength medicine, be willing to put in extra energy!

Let's talk meditation. What does meditation mean to you? Consider what comes to mind for you when you hear the word *meditation*. A lot of people picture an individual sitting in the traditional lotus position, perfectly still, legs crossed, hands on the knees, possibly even chanting the familiar, "OM," in the perfect tone. Yes, this is a form of meditation for some, and yes, this is practiced worldwide. Traditional meditation, breathwork, and yoga are all taught as forms of meditation to still the mind and calm the nervous system.

Do these work? Absolutely.

Do they work for everyone? Absolutely not.

If those methods don't work for you, I'm going to ask you to consider another definition of meditation. Maybe it doesn't have to be sitting in a lotus position. Maybe it isn't about chanting "OM," or other mantras. Maybe it isn't attending meditation classes or using a meditation app. Maybe it isn't about trying to force a stillness that doesn't want to come. Maybe it's a little more organic than that.

Let's consider meditation in broader terms.

Think about a child, for example. A child who is outside riding a bike, playing in a sandbox, or spending time alone coloring. They don't seem to have a care in the world, but they are in their own little world. During this time, their brain has time to process. It may be processing the events of the day, the week, or an event they've experienced. This may all be happening unconsciously.

For the child, this can be a form of meditation.

This happens for adults, too.

Ask yourself, *what do I like to do?* If you've forgotten what you enjoyed before life got in the way, try to remember what you liked to do once upon a time. Schedule time to try that activity. Be open to the fact that you might have to try a few things.

- Coloring – I suspect one of the reasons that adult coloring has gained such popularity in recent years is its ability to transport people to places of tranquility and meditation.

- Painting – This activity has been practiced for hundreds, if not thousands of years, as an expression of the subconscious mind.

- Baking – This simple act requires attention and focus, while contributing to a family or greater community. Many people find this to be therapeutic.

- Journaling – Journaling can offer a great release of emotion and experiences, if you allow yourself to relax into the writing and be vulnerable.

- Running – Running offers a great release for many, which not only strengthens you mentally but also physically.

- Biking – This is another physical activity many people can use to calm their nervous system.

There are countless activities that you can try, and come up with your own combination of what is effective for you.

Maybe you don't like the things you once did, and it's time to try something new. That's okay. Accept yourself for who you truly are today and be open to change. You need to find a space where meditation can happen naturally.

- **Be conscious about the unconscious.**

- **Find an activity where you can go into a meditative space.**

- **It will be transformative for you.**

I found that in the gym. In the gym, I've been able to address both the mental and physical components of my being. It has helped me to rise above my trauma. This has not happened overnight. It has taken four years. The first two were about learning to change my mindset and subsequently making a commitment. This commitment was to myself and to my health and became a journey of wellness. Initially, I went three times a week, but that wasn't a commitment. That was me saying, *I'll do it when I have time, when there's nothing better to do.*

The truth is, there's always something better to do, so this left lots of room for excuses. *I'm tired today. I didn't sleep well last night. I have had a long day. I can just go tomorrow.*

- **I had to change my mindset.**

- **If this was going to work, I had to make this a lifestyle.**

I made a conscious decision to go five days a week. It wasn't until I made a commitment that I was able to make a change. It wasn't until I committed that I learned the power of mindfulness. Every day after work, I got in my car and drove in the opposite direction from my home. I drove to the gym. There was no more mental discussion of whether I would go or have an excuse to put it off. I chose to make this part of my routine. I chose to make this part of what I do and who I am. That conscious decision marked the beginning of my transformation. I have a supportive environment where the owner cares about her clients. She has often held workshops for her members on mindfulness, meditation, and motivation.

When I enter the gym, I mentally create a space just for me. In this space, I can forget the stresses of everyday life. I leave my home life, work life, family, and friends at the door.

That hour is my time and space, where nothing else exists.

I go into a meditative space. When I do this successfully, I can push my body and my mind to reach new levels. I challenge myself mentally to push through things I once only dreamed of being able to do physically. I can process events of the day and past events on a subconscious level. This space even allows me to explore deeper levels of faith and what it means to me. In my gym time, I find the intersection of body, mind, and spirit, where I am whole. I can transcend the limiting beliefs I once held, and in doing so, I begin to reverse the effect of past traumas. Sometimes this process is conscious, and sometimes it's subconscious, but both are necessary.

In every breath and every step, I return to myself—and in that sacred return, I meet God again.

Kristina Skye, BSc. C.H.N.C., was born in the Gatineau Hills of Quebec, Canada, spending her formative years moving between Ontario, Quebec, and New York State, before settling in Calgary, Alberta, with her family at the age of 12. She attended Mount Royal University, where she obtained her Bachelor of Science degree with a major in Health Science. She then furthered her studies at the Canadian School of Natural Nutrition, becoming certified as a Holistic Nutritional Consultant. She is currently employed by a national non-profit organization, where she has worn many different hats, including working with children and serving as a community liaison between marginalized populations and other community support groups. Most recently, she serves as a Community Program Coordinator.

In addition to this, Kristina has studied the Usui System of Natural Healing to gain the distinction of Reiki Master. She also worked extensively with Angel Gold and has the honor of being one of the first Priestess initiates of the Nina Songo, Fire Heart Mystery School. She is a lifelong learner and believes that exploring the mind-body-spirit connection is the key to living a long and prosperous life.

Kristina currently lives in Calgary with her youngest son and cat and keeps herself busy by going to the gym and spending time with friends. She also loves to recharge with a cup of tea, a furry blanket, and a good book.

Connect with Kristina at:

Website: https://www.kosmicvitality.com

Email: admin@kosmicvitality.com

BE CONSCIOUS ABOUT THE UNCONSCIOUS.

~ KRISTINA SKYE

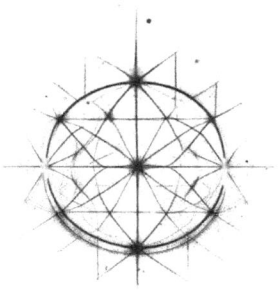

Chapter 12

WHY AVATARS SING

Resiliency Building for the Up-and-Coming Leader
Grace Kohn

My Story

Holding her legs in obvious visible pain, withering on the ground, I wondered for a moment: Is *she having a heart attack? Should I be calling 911 right now? No, I kept hearing. She is processing her grief. It's okay; everything is going to be okay. Trust your leadership.*

My friend asked me for a singing lesson—no, begged me for a singing lesson. She was all about it. "I want to take singing lessons from you. It's something I've wanted to do for a long time now. It's for me—I need to do it," she said.

"Okay, let's do it then," I replied.

And here we were, not too far into it, and I was worried something had gone incredibly wrong. Thanks to that part of us (the leader within) that seems to know what to do in times of crisis, I remained calm and encouraged her to take slow, deep, deliberate breaths.

She listened to my voice commands, "Breathe in, breathe out, breathe in, breathe out."

Slowly, she regained her composure, but her hands were still clutching her heart.

We aren't out of the woods yet, I thought.

Intuitively, I knew what was coming up for her was deep grief in her body, and even as I write this, confirmation in the form of tears rising in my eyes occurs. She's my reflection and probably yours if you're reading this.

None of us is out of the woods yet, are we? It's been an intense couple of years for everyone.

If anything, these past couple of years have thrown us around like a Raggedy Ann doll. Our nervous systems have been in a fight-or-flight mode, continuously operating in a state of fear. Who to believe and what to listen to has challenged us all. If you haven't lost one relationship over the past few years, consider yourself lucky.

"So how is singing going to help me?" you ask. "Trust my leadership," is my simple request.

It's been found that the ancients sang. They sang even before they spoke, apparently. They sang in groups and together in caves, often. The resonance they developed between themselves cemented their connection to each other and the group. Like a forest, when roots connect, information can travel quickly to all members. I bring up the woods because, as we all know, yet often forget, it's because of our tree family that we can even function on this Earth. Every time we breathe in, it's because an exchange with a tree's out-breath occurred. Whether we think about it or not, we depend on trees to keep us alive. We can do without food, even water for long periods, but a few minutes without air, baby, and you're somewhere else. Breathwork is as essential to singing as mycelium is to healthy forests. It's about connections. To become a successful leader, you must connect to your body. You hold the medicine.

Your body is intelligent. We often think all our intelligence comes from our brains. Yes, there is, of course, that type of intelligence. There is heart intelligence as well. Many organizations like HeartMath have and are proving the intelligence of the heart. Thirdly, your body has intelligence. Based on my observations, this area has received the least attention. With today's use of technology, more and more people seem to be less and less in their bodies and more in their heads. With their screens in their hands, often from morning to night, we lose our connection to our body intelligence. Singing reconnects you to that intelligence because your body is the instrument. It would be best if you were as grounded and rooted as a giant oak to sing. In fact, the more grounded you are, the more extensive your vocal range will be, the more strength your voice will have, and the more flexibility you'll have to play with sound. As we strengthen these areas, we affect how we live our lives, who we become, and how we lead.

Back to my friend, after we rebalanced her breathing, I invited her to tone some sounds. The first sound I asked her to join me in was *AH. AH,* pronounced *AWE,* is connected to our hearts. Every time we make the sound *AH,* our hearts are positively affected.

After *AH,* we played with *OH* and then *Ooo.* I recently discovered that *Noo* is an ancient word meaning primordial waters. *(*Secret Doctrine,* H.P. Blavatsky).

Ooo, pronounced as you would, the word "new" had a dramatic effect on my friend, particularly on her inner waters. Like a backed-up sink, the block in her heart area needed to be unplugged, and the miracle was that it was her very own singing voice that did just that.

The Ancients mapped out all the lines and energy centers in our bodies. Some cultures call the energy that runs through these lines and centers *chi,* and others call it *prana.* Regardless of what you call it, the bottom line is that when we get blocked in any of these areas, we have dis-ease and definite discomfort. These blocks, as I was recently reminded by my Pleiadian friend Barbara Marciniak *(*"Bringers of the Dawn"*), are primarily emotional in nature. If we're not allowed to express our emotions freely, they get backed up in the pipes. Eventually, if too much gets stuffed down there, kaboom! You have a big mess.

The ancients knew that sounding could help clear unexpressed anger, rage, sadness, guilt, and grief, and even alleviate depression. The beauty is we have the ability right inside to help ourselves. I'm happy to report my friend lived that day; I didn't call an ambulance. She walked out the door on her own accord, humming the tune of a song we worked on later that session.

Because our singing voice is so deeply connected to our soul, singing can activate powerful initiations in our body.

Just recently, another friend of mine was over for her lesson. As we made our way through various songs, we reached a point in the class where the sun was strongly streaming through a nearby window. The sun hit me first, and I immediately wanted my friend to feel it, so I led her to stand in the sun with her drum. We continued to sing. We sang a very simple song. You may even know it. It's called: *It only takes a spark to get a fire going.*

My friend is very connected to fire and leads our weekly fire gatherings. Her reason for coming for singing lessons was so she'd feel comfortable leading the women in song at the fires. It's a pleasure to teach her, as she is so open to working past her comfort zone, even if her monkey mind says she shouldn't.

As she was singing, she had an experience I'd call an initiation. It was about reconnecting parts of herself that had been split, possibly for a long time. As the words were spilling out of her mouth, she saw something in her mind's eye that penetrated her whole body deeply. She shared with me what she saw. Twenty-seven years ago, I had the same experience she was having; the only difference was that I was alone and six months pregnant.

I write in-depth about this experience in my first bestselling book, *Children of Autumn – Autism Here on Purpose.* Because I had this background, I could assist her in integrating what was going on, which has profound implications for her moving forward.

The "I" of who we are comprises different parts. There is a masculine part and a feminine part. Often, people are working primarily from one aspect. To fully become whole, we need the two parts to reunite and be in balance. The initiation my friend was having was internally reconnecting these two aspects for her. Singing was the mechanism by which this occurred. When working as our whole selves, we're far more resilient and comfortable leading.

The Medicine

Having a child with autism as well as a typical child, I've learned resiliency. There are four primary components to becoming resilient.

1. The importance of connection.
2. Wellness.
3. Healthy thinking.
4. The meaning one has with life itself.

Let's explore number one and how it relates directly to singing. To be resilient, you need to have a solid connection to yourself, others, your community, your country, Spirit, and nature. Let's go back to our beautiful tree, friends. When you're singing, I strongly recommend you think of yourself as a tree and root yourself deep into the ground. Feel that you have roots coming out the bottom of your feet, connecting with all the other trees around you. Imagine you're relating to the trees you love the most. They're all beautiful, so pick your favorite. Take some time here to feel the co-creation between you and the type of tree you've chosen. Imagine it's in front of you, and as you breathe out, you can feel it breathe in. Likewise, as it breathes out, you feel it, and you breathe in. Trees can bend to great angles. They can withstand powerful gusts of wind. Becoming connected to the Earth in the form of a tree as a place to sing from will make you more resilient in all your endeavors.

How connected to others do you feel right now? On a scale of one to ten, ten being strongly connected, where would you rate yourself? Do not go into judgment based on what you give yourself. To be resilient, you need to feel connected to others. Singing can bring this about in many ways. You can quickly join a choir, band, drumming circle, a theatre group that puts on musicals, sing with the radio, sing with your children if you have children, or join our Singing Wolves group on Monday nights. Check out www.childrenofautumn.com for more information regarding this offering.

We need to feel a connection with community, so if you cannot find something directly in your physical community, join us online. The more we build these connections, the better for us all. Everybody needs a place to howl. You are most welcome.

Did you know trees sing? Seriously. I first heard them singing in a magical place called Damanhur in northern Italy. After working with plants for over 30 years, they developed a machine that you connect to a keyboard and then connect directly to the plant. The electromagnetic field of the plant 'plays' the keyboard, or as I like to think of it, sings through the keyboard.

It's pretty amazing to witness. Once you've heard even one plant sing, it doesn't take much to imagine what an entire forest would sound like together.

Connecting to nature also improves your resiliency. If plants sing, doesn't it make even more sense to immerse yourself outside by a campfire, a body of water, or deep in a forest and sing together with the elements? Fire is such a powerful element to sing with because you have that strong sun presence with you as well. Sun gives life to all natural things and will do the same for you. As the flames dance in front of you, and while different colors paint themselves around the coals for you, sing out to the stars, moon, and all the planets. We are part of a mysterious, magnificent universe; we're here on purpose, and connecting to all these elements through song is one of the oldest and wisest ways of filling up one's battery pack.

WELLNESS AND RESILIENCY

You know you have a nervous system, but did you know it has different parts? One part is called the parasympathetic nervous system. It does its best to keep you in a relaxed state. If this system functions well, you'll feel emotionally, mentally, and physically healthier. When we're in a fight, flight, or fright mode, the sympathetic nervous system is active. Our parasympathetic nervous system kicks in and does something called down-regulating. Involved with the vagus nerve, which connects to your vocal cords and the muscles at the back of your throat, there are ways you can activate this nerve.

What can help you to down-regulate? Deep breathing, singing, and humming. It's scientifically proven that when people hum or sing, they positively affect their nervous system. Furthermore, according to Sarah Wilson, clinical neuropsychologist and head of the School of Psychological Sciences at the University of Melbourne, "There is a singing network in the brain which is quite broadly distributed. When we speak, the hemisphere of the brain dealing with language lights up. When we sing, both sides of the brain spark into life. We also see the involvement of the feeling networks of the brain."

Lastly, singing is an aerobic exercise that creates the release of endorphins. Baishali Mukherjee, the Southeast Asia regional liaison for the World Federation of Music Therapy, shares, "The feeling of happiness we get from endorphins is associated with a reduction of stress. In any situation, whether it is under stress or with any physical ailments, illness, and/or psychological deprivation, music has the potential to affect our body's immunity and mind positively."

HEALTHY THINKING AND RESILIENCY

Positive thinking, we know, affects our physiology by strengthening our immune system. To build your resiliency, sing songs of praise, inspiration, joy, gratitude, love, and communion.

LIFE MEANING

Viktor Frankl, an Auschwitz survivor, wrote a book called *Man's Search for Meaning*. He believed that humans are motivated by something he called a "Will to meaning." He argued that life could have meaning even in the most miserable circumstances and that the motivation for living comes from finding that meaning. My 93-year-old mother-in-law, who was locked in her small apartment for 21 days in complete isolation during the Canadian COVID lockdowns, found her meaning by teaching herself and singing many different hymns during those days. Her choosing this course of action kept her resilient and with us. Amazing!

This chapter aims to assist you as you evolve into the leadership role you're coded for by inspiring you to sing, hum, and practice deep breathing. The following are a few warm-up ideas for you to play with.

The ancients knew the power of sound; they are whispering to you now:

It is your birthright to sing, be proud, and change the world with your voice!

As you light up both sides of your brain, you light up the world! We need your voice. The time of the lone wolf is over. Reunite with your pack!

WARMUPS

- Breathe in through your nose and out through your mouth.

- Observe your breathing as it moves up and down your spine.

- Breathe deeply into your belly and use the Yoga child's pose. The only place you can breathe from in this position is your belly.

- Relax, and warm up your lips, blowing them together as you did as a kid. Pretend to drive a motorcycle or truck around. Let your lips really vibrate together. Move your body around if you feel inspired to. Play with the sound coming from you going up and down like a scale while you blow your lips out.

- Give your jaw a nice, gentle massage along the edges of it on both sides. Place your fingers on the edges and gently massage down to your chin. We hold a lot of stress in our jaws, so giving them a massage will feel great.

- You have three voices you can develop in your body: head, mid, and chest voice. Imagine you have a tube that is about two inches wide. It's very flexible and starts in the Earth. It comes through your body up the inside of you, like a channel, and out the top of your head. Every time you breathe in from the Earth, your breath rises through this tube, and when you make a sound, it's as if a key or a string has been played and is now resonating out through your mouth.

- Practice making the sound *AH*. When you make this sound, let your mouth drop open. Start using *AH* on any note you wish. Do this a few times, and if you can go up and down a few notes, that's great. If you have a musical instrument to use, please do. If you don't, there are numerous apps you can find to help you. VoCo, Sing Sharp, and SWIFTSCALES are a few.

- Next, experiment with *Ooo*. This sounds like "new." Play with the word *noo*. Give gratitude to a body of water you love, your favorite river, stream, creek, ocean, someone you love, or even yourself.

- Play with the sounds *Eee, OH, I,* and *A* similarly. Unmask your avatar and sing! It's your birthright.

Singer, author, advocate, speaker, teacher, mother, and now farmer, **Grace** shares tools and strategies that have helped her to remain resilient, grounded, and loving in the face of challenges. As a parent of a beautiful adult daughter living with Autism, Grace has learned many valuable lessons through her adventures. Singing since she was a toddler, she today teaches both children and adults the power of singing and how it can transform us and connect us deeply to ourselves and others. Her daughter, Julianne, went from non-verbal at seven to a non-stop singer today.

Grace is the author of the bestselling book, *Children of Autumn - Autism Here on Purpose.* She offers a unique and hopeful message that reaffirms that Autism is here on purpose to help our species evolve and become more loving. Grace has delivered her message to various audiences, including teachers, healthcare professionals, parents, and other thought leaders. Many have found personal value and relevance to their own experiences, even though they may not live with the challenge of Autism.

Grace is available for presentations to speak or sing anywhere in the world. She has presented in Canada and the United States. She lives with her Beloved in Jasper, Alberta, Canada, and recently opened the first Jule House—a unique home for special people. You can find her voice on Spotify as Griggs and Grace.

In 2022, she started the YouTube Channel "Grace, Marla, Nicole, and Friends," uniting children with nature through song, puppetry, and Drama. On this channel, children meet Elfie the Elephant and Koala, who together learn about nature, art, and our global family. If you have children or are just young at heart, you can find them on YouTube at @childrenofautumn.com.

Connect with Grace:

Website: https://childrenofautumn.com/

BE THE MIRACLE

~ GRACE KOHN

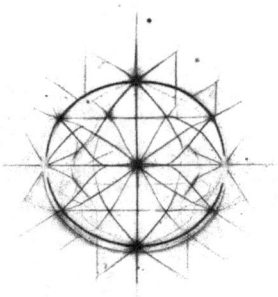

Chapter 13

TRANSFORMATION THROUGH TOUCH
When You Are Ready, Your Timeline Will Shift
Emoke Molnar

My Story

It was my turn to receive. I had everything under control.

I started to enjoy the pain, then everything shifted.

Here I am again on a different level.

I have lost control, and I am screaming my lungs out for help!

You reach a certain point in your life when you know it is time to make a decision. I remember the day when I decided to follow my intuition and chose to learn something new. I signed up for a holistic massage course, knowing I needed to take action and show up.

I signed up without even thinking.

I did not take the time to see what I had signed up for. I did not read the instructions on what to bring to class.

I just knew when to show up.

I was not prepared for what was to come.

I arrived at the class. Butterflies were dancing in my stomach. *What am I supposed to do? What's going to happen?* We were asked to share about ourselves, and at that moment, I had no idea what to say.

Oh my God! Will they be able to understand me? Is my English good enough? Who are all these people? Why do we have to share? I don't want to share! What the hell have I signed up for?

I started to see my classmates with different eyes as they shared from their hearts. *Clearly, they knew what they signed up for.* These souls gathered in this space were courageous, full of love, and wished to be in service, as did I.

I started to feel a shift in the air. My eyes locked with the man sitting across the circle from me. *I know you will be my first partner.* I smiled as we were paired. *I wonder how many more times that is going to happen this week?* I thought as he started to practice on me.

My childhood memories started to poke into my consciousness as he worked through the teachings.

What is that mark on your head?

Are you strong enough to wear the name they are calling you?

Your mind is endless.

I see the gypsy woman who told me I am marked.

I see my mother throwing my Tarot decks into the fire.

Who am I? Why am I thinking about all these things?

Am I a witch, as the gypsy woman said?

As the lesson continued, I didn't have time to integrate what I had just experienced. Now, the tables had turned, and I was the one giving the massage.

I began to relax and enjoy the process of learning, and I was utterly amazed at how complex our bodies are. I wanted to absorb the teachings from these masters, even though I didn't understand what was happening.

My turn on the table again! Not sure how I feel about this!

There I was, back on the table, the first in the class to start crying.

I'm so embarrassed! I don't want to cry! I'm so emotional.

I can't wait for this day to be over!

Will my warrior survive this?

My partner was massaging my knees, and I was thrust back in time to my father's funeral.

Why am I back at my father's funeral?

What am I doing here? There is death all around me!

"Breathe, breathe," I heard the teacher step in and whisper in my ear. "Come back," she whispered as she called me back to the present. I was safe. I did not need to fear death here. The poor guy working on me had no idea what was happening.

With the second day over, I was happy and relaxed. I survived day two! I would not be so lucky the next day. I did not survive day three.

I'm losing my legs! Who is putting hot stones on my legs? Why isn't anyone helping me?! I feel myself leaving my body, and I witness my anguish from the corner of the ceiling.

What is happening?

There are five people around the massage table. Someone is dying on the table, and nobody is helping. *Does that person have no soul? Wait a minute, that's me! That's my body! I must go back to it. How do I get back to it?*

"Help me before I lose my legs!" I begged my teacher. "Something is on my legs!"

"There is nothing on your legs; just breathe, breathe, breathe," she says as I feel myself drop back into my body.

I open my eyes to witness my teachers surrounding me. *I'm so confused.*

I don't understand what is happening.

I feel an energy with a purple light rushing through my body.

Trying to kill me.

Is this the end of my life?

Screaming, crying, *God, stop it before I die!*

Finally, I get a minute to breathe and rest into full bliss as my body starts to surrender. I allow my muscles to sink into the bed as my heart and breath slow down into stillness. Suddenly, my senses become heightened as paralysis takes over my body.

Wait!

What's happening?

Oh no, here it comes again!

My breath quickens as the purple wave hits me again, ripping up my spine and out of the top of my head, I'm on fire! This rollercoaster of energy dominates me.

I am burning alive!

I can't catch my breath,

I have nothing left to scream with!

The burning sensation coursing through my body is both strange and familiar.

I think to myself, *Is my blood boiling in my veins? Am I being boiled alive?*

At the same time, my body is floating on the bed.

Finally, I trust and surrender to the process. I let the energy take over, and I enjoy the ride.

That day, I let everything go on that table.

I understood; nothing was in my hands anymore.

As the class ended on that memorable third day, and everyone slowly left our sacred space, I rested in the stillness, not wanting to move.

Before I left, one of the teachers slipped a folded piece of paper into my hand. When I finally opened the paper, the words "Kundalini awakening" were scribbled on it.

I left the class, glad to see the sun as I walked home. *How did I get home? How did I unlock my door? Who put the clothes on my floor? What is a Kundalini awakening?*

I went to bed feeling tired and happy.

I got another chance to live.

I woke up in the middle of the night, terrified. I was experiencing the same energy that was present in class today, but now the energy came with a blinding white light. I was scared to be alone in my place with the thoughts in my mind.

I am alone here.

I will die this time, and nobody will know.

I surrendered to the experience and chose to face whatever shadows showed up.

I started to feel my body. *Am I dreaming? Am I in life? Am I dead?*

The experience had me questioning everything in life. I chose to get up and shift the energy. As I drank my water, my attention turned to the paper on my table that my teacher handed me. I researched what a Kundalini awakening meant. I had never heard of it before. I found all the information that resonated with my experience, but left me with even more questions.

The next day, I experienced a shift. I was no longer counting the days anymore, as I had let control go and enjoyed the energy I was receiving instead. Everyone wanted to know what happened and what I felt, but I had no words for them. I only wished for all of them to have the same experience I had.

I did not sleep for days, lost in my new little world.

On the last day of the course, we were asked to invite someone we could work on for the exam. I asked one of my friends to come and be my first victim. The massage was going well when suddenly I noticed that all my teachers were in my room.

Why are you all here?

Is something going to happen?

The massage is almost over!

I asked my friend to flip over on her back, so I could work on her belly. I was overwhelmed with emotion, and I started to cry. Angel appeared beside me and put her hand on top of mine, pressing it into my friend's belly.

"Look at me. You can do it. You got this."

She steps back, and I hear Angel's voice: *You can do it.*

I felt stronger and understood. *Yes, I can do it.*

I stopped crying, grounded myself, and the energy shifted.

My friend started to have an emotional release as I maintained the pressure on her belly. I stayed present with her, as that's what I needed when I went through the same thing earlier. I knew she was dealing with her stuff, and I knew I wouldn't leave her while she was doing it.

It didn't take long for her to surrender and trust the process. I couldn't believe I was witnessing my friend having an emotional release right before my eyes. I then realized you can control anything, no matter how strong (or not) you think you are.

She started to take a deep breath. "What happened? I don't remember," she questioned, dropping back into her body.

Holding her hand, I shared with her, "You were ready to let some things go." She felt light and happy after our session was over. "Thank you for being there for me, Emoke," she replied.

It was an intense experience to hold space and facilitate my first emotional release, while being assisted by Angel. I felt happy and strong, knowing I had someone who could step in and help.

Since that day, my life has shifted in amazing ways and different directions. I never thought I would be serving humanity the way I am today. The deep work I learned and experienced within that course helped me to see and understand more about the human body, energy, and emotional blockage.

This modality allowed me to gain deeper connections with a higher spirit and the universe. Many thanks to my teachers for having the patience to help me understand how to trust my intuition. I appreciate them for pushing me through the leftover residual blockages and helping me start my new journey.

After completing the course, I felt the calling for my new life to start. I started doing massages, and a whole new world opened up for me.

One surprise after another became my normal. I stepped into the flow of my new life. I still don't always understand what's happening through my touch and what I'm able to do. I choose to follow my intuition, and with pure intention, I know that I can trust it.

I became curious about energy work and did some Reiki courses to have more understanding of what I was doing. I always stayed connected with my teachers in case I had questions.

One day, Angel and I decided to exchange a massage. She came to my space and while facilitating her massage I had a vision, a feeling. I felt the door open, and someone came into the room and stood by the door. As I was describing this presence, how it looked, what it was wearing, and what it was saying, she just listened.

"This is interesting," she replied. This spirit stayed there the whole time, as if it was assisting my job or holding space for her. As I was finishing, the spirit left. After the massage, she pulled out her phone and showed me a person who was one of her mentors. Wow, she was exactly who I saw. "Isn't it interesting? I don't understand how that could happen!" I exclaimed.

"Emoke, not all humans with long hair are females," Angel replied.

What is happening? I do not understand!

How is this possible to see them? What do they want?

Why are they here?

"How far are you with your Reiki training?" Angel asked.

"I'm ready for my Master attunement, as I'm doing more than I have ever imagined. I'm ready!"

"Let's do it!"

The day came, and we made our way up the side of the dormant volcano at the edge of the city. Listening to the call of the sacred space, I found a ridge with a rock that could be used as a chair. I got comfortable, and Angel started the ritual.

I found myself following the wind to my childhood graveyard in Transylvania.

I was participating in a ceremony with my relatives on Hallows Eve. I was visiting the deathbeds of my deceased relatives and celebrating them with prayer and candlelight, when I heard Angel calling my name.

As I dropped back into my body, I remembered being surrounded by shamans. Then, an eagle's eye came right to my face, to my eye, and blinked into my soul.

Angel translated what I did into words I understood. We shared deep conversations about what a channel is and about tools to help us open our channel. We hold all the keys within.

She encouraged me to trust and keep going. "Do not be afraid, and the right help will always show up when you need it."

I keep sharing my gifts, and it gets easier to tune in and receive more guidance. The teachings were deep, and I went through a spiritual awakening during this process. I learned to let things go, and now I understand the benefits this work has for your health and body.

It is an amazing feeling to be able to help others on their own journey of transformation.

Finally, I understand: "When the student is ready, the right teacher will show up."

The Medicine

We are taught how to be mad, resentful, and how to hold onto these negative emotions and other things that no longer serve us.

We hang onto people and experiences from long ago that don't exist in our world anymore. We have never been taught how to let things go.

Letting things go is not easy. It's a lot of work. It's our life's work; it never ends. But it's worth every minute when we decide we want to change our lives.

The medicine is in you. We can't change anything or anybody, except our own thoughts, patterns, and our view of life.

As soon as a trigger shows up, here are a few questions to ask yourself:

- What are you holding onto?

- Why are you holding onto it?

- Where do you feel the pain? Is the pain familiar?

- Let all the answers come to you, experience them with emotion, and stay with yourself as you process the experience that shows up.

- Forgive yourself and the experience.

- Let it go! If you wait, it will be harder to do later.

You'll feel amazing the minute things shift and will want to continue doing it. As you start to teach your body, heart, and mind to let go, it gets easier.

You will want to see what's behind all the doors of your soul. You will want to clean out all that does not serve you, because you will begin to understand you do not need it. Waiting can have detrimental effects on your health.

From my own experience, the first breakthrough is the hardest. Then, you're gifted with the key to unlocking your heart and soul.

Having experienced true transformation myself, I know how hard it is to let things go. We create different stories for the underlying issues that keep us stuck. People wait too long to release their pain. There is no point in holding anger, grief, or pain anymore.

Stop the addiction to suffering.

Most of us are never lucky enough to meet someone who can help us see and realize all the garbage we're carrying. I am grateful for the teachers who walked with me on my path and gave me the tools to now help others.

I'm encouraging you to be open and curious. Be open to change in your life and be willing to receive the help you deserve. I know the usual is so convenient, even if it's painful, because the unknown is so scary. But are you really happy with the life you have right now?

As soon as you are ready for the unknown, it will show itself to you, and it is beautiful.

Emoke is a skilled massage and bodywork practitioner from the Raynor Naturopathic School of Massage and Bodywork.

Her work with Angel has allowed her the honor of being one of the first Priestess initiates of the Nina Songo, Fire Heart Mystery School, and Reiki Master through the Usui System of Natural Healing.

In her free time, you can find her climbing mountains, swimming in lakes, and creating magical herbal medicine in her kitchen.

Connect with Emoke:

Email: mocike13@gmail.com

Facebook: https://www.facebook.com/emoke.molnar.583

THE MEDICINE IS IN YOU. WE CAN'T CHANGE ANYTHING OR
ANYBODY, EXCEPT OUR OWN THOUGHTS, PATTERNS,
AND OUR VIEW OF LIFE.

~ EMOKE MOLNAR

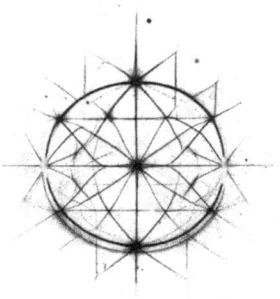

Chapter 14

SADDLING THE HEART

A Journey Back Through the Soul

Dustin Kaiser

My Story

Most of this life, I rode alone.

From high desert mountains to the valleys below, through the depths of my heart and the shadows of my past,

I rode through life way too fast.

Not paying attention to things as they come, reaching for alcohol to help me feel numb.

I relied on a bottle to hide behind my heart,

a drink or two every night, so my feelings would not start.

I was a tough cowboy, I played the part, riding wild horses from dawn till dark.

Pushing cattle to places they didn't want to go, this is how I used to feed my wild soul.

I tip my hat to shield my face from the freezing northern wind as the snow pushes across my rose-colored cheeks. I kick my horse into a trot, trying to get to the shelter sooner. I try to keep a perfect cadence, so he does not lose his footing and slip on the ice-covered desert floor. I swing my leg over the saddle, stepping off my horse to fix the broken fence. My boots sink down into the fresh-fallen snow. Suddenly, I find myself dropping to my knees, tears flowing from my eyes, as flashbacks from my four-wheeler accident come barreling through me like a motion picture. This was the moment I died at age 18, when I met my Creator and was given a choice.

Am I going to fulfill my life's purpose?

Am I going to start over again?

Is it time for me to let go and start a new life cycle?

I want to stay on Earth.
I know I can be happy here.

I choose to stay.

I set my soul on fire.

I open my heart to let it all go. I opened my hands to guide me to the light.

Help me, Lord, this cowboy has no more fight.

The messages echoed through my soul from the different teachers who came to me from my past, guiding and holding me in love. Then, like a crack of thunder from up above:

This is the day I let it all go.

This is the day I bury it in the cold winter snow.

This will be your Ego's last ride.

I'm here today writing this chapter, hoping this gives you the courage, heart, and guidance to follow your soul's true purpose. It was a rough road for this cowboy. I battled right out of high school with depression and suicide, alcohol addiction, married and divorced with a DUI before I was 21 years old.

I had enough! I knew I must turn my life around. I loaded up my saddle and headed for Nevada to cowboy on the big ranches and figure out this life purpose I was supposed to learn. The next few years, I traveled from ranch to ranch through Nevada, and up through Montana chasing greener grass, bigger pastures, and new mountains to ride, trying to find something to keep me alive, buried in a bottle of booze, keeping me from feeling my feelings. Alcohol was the only thing that made me think I fit in with the other cowboys. I knew in the depths of my soul that I was here for something bigger.

Why would I get a second chance?

I sure as hell was not meant to be a whiskey-drunk, saddle tramp.

I've always practiced saying yes to an opportunity to face the unknown. It's one of my greatest thrills. That's how I ended up in northern British Columbia. That's where I met my first teacher, a local elder from the tribe up north who showed up at the ranch where I was working that day. The moment he got out of his truck, our souls connected as we talked about hunting. Little did I know, the thing he was hunting was my own soul.

Who is this guy? He feels so familiar.

I knew in my heart that he was there to help me. "Would you be interested in me doing some healing work on you?" he offered. Without hesitation, I said, "Yes!"

As he placed his hands on my bare chest, I could smell the Palo Santo he burned. This was something so new to me, but so familiar. Something I've smelled my entire life, but I've never heard of. He moved energy and worked on my eyes. Opening up my heart chakra, he removed ancestral blockages. It was one of the most amazing experiences I've ever felt in my life. Our session started to come to a close, and I fluttered to open my eyes. I could see him lean over me, his hands on my chest, sweat running down his face, a big grin on his face, looking into my soul. He told me, "You know that you're supposed to be doing this, right?"

With a big sheepish grin and no words on my lips, my heart answered the call. I didn't even have a clue what 'this' was. I knew how to ride broncs and push cows; that is what I knew. This new energy poured through every part of my body. Just like Palo Santo, so strange but so familiar. This ignited a fire deep in my soul, and I wanted to dive in for more!

I was lucky enough to work with him often throughout the summer before I went back down to the States. I couldn't handle the frozen northern country anymore, so I headed to California, which was a hell of a lot warmer.

California is where I met the love of my life.
A beautiful blonde cowgirl that someday, I would call my wife.
Little did I know this cowgirl would play a part in the settling of my wild heart.

Our summer started off in love,
with many nights staring at the stars above.
Speaking of dreams and manifestation, talking about silly cowboy meditations.

Summer came and summer went, and that fall I got into a wreck.
Shattered my leg from my knee to my toes,
this is where opportunity arose.

April found a therapy called Bowen two years prior;
she'd already been goin'.
It helped her with her muscles; it helped her stay on track. It kept her moving forward, from horse wrecks a while back.

It came to me one night in the dream, it came to me like it was meant to be.
When the words "Learn Bowen" echoed through my soul!
This is where my medicine would grow.
I followed the schooling through and through, finishing what I started like cowboys do.
Letting my hands guide the way,
I had no clue where this would take me someday.

As the grass started to grow, it was time for us to go.
We moved to Oregon; this is where my deep healing really began.

I took a job at a high mountain ranch.
Living that far from town will surely give a cowboy a chance to sit in the evenings and talk about cowboy romance.

Now, cowboy romance, you see, it's not what you might think it to be.
I'm not talking about a night on the town,
I'm talking about sitting with your feelings when no one's around.
Sitting on top of an icy ridge waiting for the sun to rise will sure give a cowboy time to sit and think and feel wise.

Watching the deer in the meadows below,
Who else can sit atop a horse and get their chakras to glow!
Now these are things I used to keep to myself, for I didn't need the other cowboys getting roused. So, you see, talking romance was different for me.

April would give me the chance that I need to walk into our house, to sing, and to dance.
She would hold the space for me; she gave me the chance to just be. . .

We would speak of things so deep and so true.
We would share pieces of medicine that we both knew.
Chakras, stones, and sticks, moving energy with the flick of the wrist.
Healing our traumas, we would share from our past,
releasing the things that no longer last.
We are twin flames that have finally crossed paths.

The more time we spent together, the more we did shift. As we both continue to walk into our own special gifts.

Summer had come and winter went,
it was time for us to travel living out of our cowboy tent.

Looking for new work to do, something cowboys are accustomed to.
But this time was different, you see, this time I had a partner with me.

We had a lot of fun that summer, traveling from ranch to ranch.
Trying to find that special place where we could hang our hats.

We traveled through Tehachapi,
then over to Nevada across that Sagebrush Sea.
Checked out a ranch near Salt Lake City, there were
too many people for me.
None of those ranches made our hearts dance,
so we packed up our saddles, giving Oregon another chance.

As it started to get cold and I came to my senses,
I finally realized I was done riding these old damn fences.
As I picked myself up from the snow-covered floor, I knew I would not
be riding these broncs anymore. I climbed on my horse and
straddled my saddle,
trotting back home to tell my wife about this epic battle.
As we lay in bed later that evening,
I put down the book that I had been reading.
I told her what happened that day, I told her that it would all be okay!
She looked at me with a great big grin and said,
"This is where your medicine begins."

The Medicine

When we begin our walks through our inner journeys, this can be a very dark and lonely time of releasing and surrendering, but as we continue to walk through this path and work through our shadows, the reward on the other side is pure bliss—you start to align with your soul's true purpose. Here are some helpful tools I've picked up along the way.

ALLOW YOURSELF TO DIE

This is the moment when you hit that breaking point that can be referred to as rock bottom. When you're in that space and decide to make a change, one thing you can do is sit down and make a list of five things you want to rebirth in your new life. Examples are love, abundance, health, spirituality, well-being, commitment, or whatever your heart may desire. Write these things down somewhere where you can see them daily so you can start creating that new story of rebirthing your new life.

RELEASE EVERYTHING

One way to practice this is to write a letter to all the people or things that have gotten you to the point where you are today. The point of releasing and falling back in love with yourself. This letter is to take your power back! You can be as aggressive or meaningful as you need to be. Remember, the point of this is to let it all go! Then burn it. Hold yourself in a sacred ceremony while releasing all the things written in this letter that are no longer part of your story.

SURRENDER

Surrender to yourself. Sit alone with yourself. Take time to accept that sometimes life is unfair. Sometimes life is painful and overwhelming. Take time to be honest with yourself. Start dealing with your own emotions. You can't run from them, and you can't avoid them any longer. It's time to surrender to yourself. Love yourself and who you truly are!

DROP YOUR EGO

This can be a very hard thing as we move forward in our journeys. Sometimes our ego is our identity. It's who we have created, but it does not align with our true divine selves. Here are a few ways to help you drop your ego and connect with your divine soul purpose:

Be in a state of openness. You can't learn if you think you already know.

Release your pride. It's okay to need others. Be open to love and acceptance of abundance.

Connect with nature. Take off your boots and connect to Mother Earth. Tell her all of the things you're ready to release and let her take that energy that no longer serves you.

Start loving yourself. Listen to yourself and fall back in love with the things that help you to make your medicine. Make time to take care of yourself.

One other thing that can be a very powerful tool through this journey of releasing things is to write your own eulogy. Sit down and talk with yourself. You will find the things that truly matter in your life when you decide to let it all go.

Because with every death comes rebirth; this is our time to shine! As we have no more attachments to the things that never mattered in the first place. We are in line with our true divine selves. Loving ourselves and others can be the greatest medicine of all.

A near death experience combined with the bumps, bruises, and broken bones that come from a lifetime of long days in the saddle tending to cattle and training young horses, **Dustin** was guided into alternative medicine in search of living a pain-free and natural lifestyle. Diving deep into the spiritual well-being and the retrieval of his own soul. Opening his heart to help others experience the same opportunities, Buckaroo Buddha Holistic Healing LLC was established in 2019 by April and Dustin Kaiser. Building a bridge for the ranching community and those alike, providing physical, mental, and spiritual well-being. Peace, health, and cowboy shit.

- Bowen Therapy Specialist
- Shamanic Master Reiki Energy Healing and Ceremony
- Soul Retrieval
- Activation Breathwork

Connect with Dustin:

Email: buckaroobuddha1111@gmail.com

Website: https://www.buckaroobuddha.com

LinkedIn: https://www.linkedin.com/in/buckaroo-buddha-4137a2232/

Facebook: https://www.facebook.com/buckaroobuddha1111

Instagram: https://www.instagram.com/buckaroobuddha1111/

A SPIRITUAL JOURNEY IS LIKE RIDING A FRESH COLT.
SOMETIMES YOU'RE GOING TO GET YOUR GUTS STOMPED ON.
BUT AS YOU PROGRESS THROUGH YOUR JOURNEY,
YOU LEARN TO RIDE WITH PRESENCE,
PERFECT CADENCE, AND FLOW.

LIFE: TAKE A DEEP SEAT.

~ DUSTIN KAISER

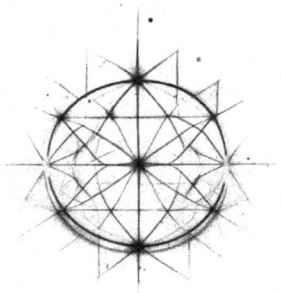

Chapter 15

THE HORSEHEAD CLAUSE

I Will Never Again Negotiate with Potential
Angel Gold

𝕸y 𝕾t⊕ry

I keep hurting you, and I'm not interested in changing the way I show up.

The first time I met Seth, he carried his charm like a backstage pass, certain it would grant him access to whatever spotlight he thought he deserved.

The desert heat of Teotihuacán shimmered around us that day, and I felt the ancient stones vibrate beneath my bare feet.

He told me he was on a pilgrimage, chasing truth. I believed him, because back then, truth was a romantic word that felt warm in my mouth. He smiled, quoted fragments of spiritual teachings while he stared deep into my eyes, and said the right things about spirit and service.

I let the melody override the tremor in my gut that whispered, *Wait*. To the jaguar-shaped cloud drifting above the pyramid of the Sun, I promised: *If this is love, I will honor it.*

I didn't yet know the difference between honoring love and hemorrhaging self.

In the two years that followed, we wrote a book together—*Bytes of Light*—braiding his tales of cosmic epiphany with my own wolf-medicine origin story. His chapter two, "Anchored in Truth," read like prophecy: a man leaving his marriage because loyalty weighed more than freedom.

I edited his words late at night, marking passages where he praised honesty but refused accountability. My throat tightened, yet I chalked it up to, *I'm not quite healed from my hysterectomy and the trauma induced during that time.*

Meanwhile, we filmed podcasts, hosted breathwork circles, fell asleep on beds of borrowed Airbnb's as we travelled the world, and told each other we were twin flames. He called me his love; I called him my alpha, mirrors, as he was the closest mirror I found to date that matched my alpha within.

Mirrors, I learned, can also be funhouse glass, stretching, shrinking, distorting until you no longer recognize the original face. But the truth was, I never knew his original face. The truth was, he chose to put on a mask and "try on" my way of living. He had no idea what being a true alpha meant.

The fracture began not with betrayal that happened in Teotihuacán, but with a bargain: "Let's pause the romance so we can focus on creation."

He commented, "I can't be the partner you need, but we can still be roommates. We cohabitate so well, and I love the life we created with our puppies. We can still be business partners and lovers when it feels light. I can commit to sexual monogamy, but that's it." I remember sitting around the fire pit in our backyard, with the sun streaming rays of light into my soul, thinking: *Did he just say that?*

I wasn't sure whether to scream, laugh, or crumble.

But my body answered before my mind could make meaning.
I froze. Time stood still as the sun rays beat down on me.
Like the part of the wild animal that knows, this is the moment you either die or decide.

Something cracked.

Not just in our relationship, but in my internal compass.

Because how do you continue to cohabitate with someone who admits they're willing to keep harming you, just so long as they're not held accountable for the wound?

And that's when the clause was born, not yet in words, not yet in wisdom, but as a quiet, internal scream:

"There must be a boundary strong enough
to hold the magic without letting it maim you."

Because the love was magical.
The sex was sacred.
The connection was undeniable.
But the soul contract collapsed.

And what he offered me at that moment wasn't a relationship.
It was a performance of partnership, without the presence of it.

What he proposed was this:
Let me keep access to your body, your gifts, your warmth, your loyalty, but let me be free of your needs.

He wanted the *ritual* without responsibility.
The *medicine* without the *mirror.*
The *power* without the *price* of true intimacy.

My chest felt hollow, but I said, "I need time to think." As the months passed, the poison crept into the house.

I thought compromise was compassion. Compromise meant I was a "good spiritual girl." *Polyamory is a thing in some communities;* I told myself when my nervous system built a wildfire. I thought staying close meant staying safe. My nervous system understood differently; it braced, storing receipts of every micro abandonment as he continued to flirt, calling it harmless, especially with my best friend.

Grief arrived as rage. It howled through every cell that once softened to fit his contour.

I left our shared home after the most devastating week I can remember. Witnessing him provide a course to the fire department we were supposed to do together; saying goodbye and putting to rest our family cat; and performing Christmas for the kids with fake smiles and heart-crushing moments where none of us were allowed emotional closure for fear of making the man in the house uncomfortable. I didn't say goodbye to King Thomas (our cat) metaphorically. Not symbolically.

Literally—he was euthanized.
King Thomas died like a monarch.

Not rushed. Not afraid. Not alone. He lay in state for hours, his purring chest slowing to silence, his body held between two guardians—his dad and me—as he drifted between worlds.

King Thomas and I shared clairvoyance like I had with no other animal. He showed me the children. All of them.

The ones who clung to his fur during couch naps, the ones who whispered secrets into his ears, the ones who never got to say goodbye with words. He showed me his mothers. Not just the biological one—the goddesses who loved fiercely, even if they didn't stay. The ones who kept showing up until it cost them too much to remain as well.

And then he showed me sovereignty.
Mine.
It came not as a crown, but as a stare. That famous feline stare—ancient, unimpressed, unapologetically regal. Stalk your sovereignty, he said.

That cat was more than a pet. He was a witness.
A soft-bodied keeper of the household's secrets.

He curled in the laps of every woman who mothered those children.
He watched us dream the dream together.
He watched it die.

And when he passed, something else passed with him.
A spell. A structure. A story.

I left, hearing, "I get the gold medal for smooth divorces."

I carried something no man could take from me again as I walked out the door:
A sacred no.
A holy clause.
A line drawn in mythic gold.

I got in my vehicle, with the flames of his destruction encoded on my license plate and the Maltese Cross stuck to my back window. A symbol of protection and honor. A symbol worn by those who dedicate their lives to serving and saving others. A symbol I used to wear to bed, dressed in his shirt. The shirt I left ruffled in a pile on the floor of his bedroom on the day I left.

The day I left, fresh snow fell outside. Each flake was a contract I didn't sign.

I drove north to the Okanagan, across the border, to the land that birthed me, to a den, deep in the mountains overlooking a knife-quiet lake. There, I listened to the silence until it spoke:

The wound isn't that he chose elsewhere.
The wound is that you chose less.

I wrote that sentence over and over until my pen shredded the page.

Memories surfaced: all the breakfasts I cooked, the business he left for me to run by myself, the moves I didn't want, the edges of the mountains we nearly died on because of his risky choices. The abandonment two days after my hysterectomy, to go play with his friends on the river, repeating the same pattern with another woman two months after I left.

I recalled how he praised my resilience the way a miner praises a canary—an instrument for his survival.

In my new den's dim light, I decided: *I will no longer be anyone's canary, concubine, or convenient caregiver.*

"Concubine: a woman who cohabits with a man to whom she is not legally married, especially one regarded as socially or sexually subservient; mistress. (among polygamous peoples) a secondary wife, usually of inferior rank." ~Dictionary.com

I asked the lake to witness. It answered with a single ripple, as if nodding.

Three months later, we met on Zoom for what I hoped would be a closure conversation. He wanted ease; I wanted an earthquake.

When I mentioned his pattern of leaving wives and immediately jumping into new beds, betrayal with no repair, and wanting to keep benefits, he smirked. "You're too intense."

"I only want to remain friends if it doesn't require work."

The mirror cracked clean then; *intensity* is another word for truth when truth offends the comfortable.

I told him I was writing a chapter about my experience. He laughed. I didn't.

The laugh lingered between us like smoke from a cheap incense stick— sweet at first whiff, toxic when inhaled too long.

"Is that a threat?" His grin turned to dark stone, and my body reacted with a full hive breakout, two visits to the ER that week, and a trip to see my family for support.

The energetic tendrils of our connection remained, reflections given and space held for repair, a map to follow for repair with no reciprocity.

I booked a haircut for July 2, his birthday. Ritual: cut the cords at their source.

The scissors became a spell. Each lock that fell was a shedding of roles I no longer need to play, of hopes that no longer hold me, of a version of me that stayed too long in a love that couldn't hold its shape.

This wasn't vanity
This was ceremony
A sacred severing
A rebirth
A becoming

The stylist was the partner of the man who once dyed my hair for the Phoenix ritual before Teotihuacán; the symmetry felt surgical. As locks fell, I imagined every strand a story in which I dimmed so he could shine. Freshly shorn, I looked in the mirror and finally saw my own eyes, unblurred by compromise.

The jaguar was there, sleek and certain.

Back home, I reread his chapter in *Bytes of Light*, "Anchored in Truth." The irony pulsed. His chapter celebrated leaving a woman who demanded loyalty; my new chapter would show the sequel.

Him refusing loyalty again, this time to me.

Cycles repeat until someone chooses the taller timeline. It would be me.

I turned on a lamp made of salt and began typing.

The Horsehead Clause unfurled sentence by sentence.

A declaration that I'd never again negotiate with potential.

Love, in my kingdom, requires provision, repair, and reciprocity.

I wrote until dawn, words spilling like phoenix feathers across the screen.

When I finished, I stepped outside. The sky was soft violet, a threshold hue. Birds were already busy, not waiting for permission to sing. I realized I, too, was busy—building worthiness, forging vision, refusing to orbit anyone who mistook me for free light.

The chapter was born.

Somewhere, a man might skim it and think I sound bitter. Let him. Bitterness is unmetabolized truth; I metabolized mine into medicine.

And medicine, once brewed, belongs not to the wound maker but to the world.

Invocation

I revoke my participation in the economy of almost.
I am not a reward for potential.
My love is not available for layaway.
Access to me requires offering. Real. Tangible. Offering.

What does "provision" mean to you?

You used to say yes to possibility. Now, you say yes to provision.
Not just money, but effort, stability, repair, emotional integrity, spiritual congruence.

The capacity to provide something of substance. Something that feeds your nervous system, not just your ego. That nourishes your body, not just your fantasies.

Provision isn't transactional—it's sacred.

It says: I bring value to the altar, because I revere what I'm asking to touch.

Most men were taught proximity is contribution.

That showing up with vibes, attention, and a Spotify playlist is enough to earn sex, support, and soul.

They're not used to being asked for more. But more is what's required now.

A man who flinches when you ask for something real doesn't love you;

he loves the benefits of you.

The healing. The affection. The inspiration.
The unpaid labor. The goddess's energy.
The emotional CPR. The sex.
The soul-food. The aesthetic. The convenience.

You aren't the warming station while he looks for his trophy.
You aren't the therapist while he avoids his shadow.
You aren't the priestess he drains to feel divine.

You are the altar. And the altar doesn't beg.
So now, if someone wants access to you, your time, your temple, your tenderness, they must bring something.
Provision is the new love language.
Not in the patriarchal sense of domination or dependence.
But in the sacred sense of mutuality.

It means:

- He repairs what he ruptures.
- He offers energy that makes your body feel safer, not more alert.
- He shows up when it's hard, not just when it's hot.
- He contributes, not just consumes.

Provision is not about being kept. It's about being met.

And if they cannot meet you, they don't get to keep orbiting.

You are not the satellite wife of someone else's rising self.

Are you ready to integrate this medicine fully?

☩HE 𝔐EDICINE

THE HORSEHEAD CLAUSE: A TOOL FOR SACRED SEPARATION

The Horsehead Clause is a sovereign boundary agreement you make with yourself. It exists to protect your body, your brilliance, and your becoming from anyone who wants access without accountability, affection without attunement, and intimacy without integrity.

It says:

> "You do not get to keep my energy, my gifts,
> or my body once you've named yourself a source of harm.
> You may go in peace, but you may not stay in power."

It's not punishment.
It's protection.
It's not dramatic.
It's devotional.
It is the line between love and self-abandonment.
It is the clause that breaks the spell.

HOW IT WORKS

You invoke the clause when:

- Someone confesses to harming you and shows no desire to change.
- You're being used for your gifts while being denied your needs.
- You're offered connection, but only on terms that exclude your full humanity.
- Love becomes a performance, not a presence.
- You're asked to continue the relationship without repair.

The clause isn't about ultimatums.
It's about truth.

It says:

> *"I believe you. I believe you when you say you don't want to grow.*
> *So, I'll grow without you."*

RITUAL: WRITE YOUR OWN CLAUSE

1. Light a candle.
2. Write this heading at the top of the page:
   "If you want my light, you must. . ."
3. Complete the sentence. Be fierce. Be precise. Be sovereign.
4. Then write:
   "If you refuse, you may go in peace. But you may not stay in power."
5. Read it aloud.
6. Burn it. Or fold it into your journal as a talisman.

This is not a threat.
It is a *prayer of protection* for your future self.

JOURNAL PROMPTS

- Where have I allowed continued access to someone who refused to repair the rupture they caused?
- What part of me still thinks love requires suffering?
- What does provision mean to me now—not just in money, but in energy, presence, consistency, and repair?

The Horsehead Clause is more than a boundary; it's a blueprint.

If this chapter sliced something open, the eBook would salt, soothe, and spell it shut.

- Includes: The full clause, red-flag scanner, exit scripts, self-repair rituals, and a soul contract revocation ceremony.
- Download it here:
  https://www.skool.com/fire-heart-mystery-school/classroom

You don't need to be burned again to finally draw the line.

This time, you get to leave the offering. Not be it.

I saw the clause I wrote wasn't just about boundaries.
It was about initiation.
I wasn't just leaving a man.
I was leaving the part of me who believed love required my suffering.
I wasn't just walking away.
I was walking as a woman who could be trusted with her own knowing.
Finally.
Fully.

King Thomas crossed the rainbow bridge.
I crossed my own. And birthed medicine for my new world.

HORSEHEAD SPELL

"No contribution, no access. No offering, no opening.
I revoke all contracts with charisma.
I require evidence. I require energy. I require provision."

(Repeat as needed when ghosts text. Or when your body starts to crave scraps.)

Want the full eBook?

Get it in the Fire Heart Mystery School, free Library, and start anchoring your own boundaries now:

https://www.skool.com/fire-heart-mystery-school/classroom

Get your eBook, stay for community and support.

INVOCATION

I REVOKE MY PARTICIPATION IN THE ECONOMY OF ALMOST.
I AM NOT A REWARD FOR POTENTIAL.
MY LOVE IS NOT AVAILABLE FOR LAYAWAY.
ACCESS TO ME REQUIRES OFFERING. REAL. TANGIBLE. OFFERING.

~ANGEL GOLD

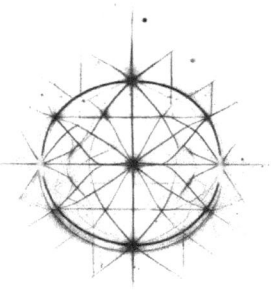

Chapter 16

RIDING THROUGH THE FIRE

A Cocoon's Journey in Search of Heaven on Earth

April Kaiser

My Story

The ways in which my ancestors set me up to gallop through fires in their own unique and private way is the gratitude I hold in every ceremony today. Magical helpers were dotted throughout my younger years as breadcrumbs on my journey to awareness. Looking back now, I'm able to see, for example, how my grandmother played an important role in the protection of my birth. She helped cure the spiritual glitch we're both aware of and has now taken from me the cross that I bear, breaking a generational curse.

My aunt completed her part, communicating with me and expressing in great detail how this glitch came to be. This confirmation validated my experience and fortified my path forward. An adopted mother gave me the tools to survive in this life, deepening my warrior goddess. My grandfather appeared through a psychic gypsy healer, expressing to me the importance of severing every single one of my relationships. These are some of the huge clues along my personal path that I've held onto for continued medicine.

Humans are domesticated by control. Control is what holds us in cages of thoughts fed to us by authority. Often, we don't attempt to question out of fear of punishment, such as removing personal rights to free will.

This may sound severe to some, but others will know what I'm speaking of. These things were made very clear to me as a young child raised in an authoritative family, within an extreme religious organization. Guilt is one tool used to gain more control. "If you were to leave God's one and only true religion, your example would turn others away. Therefore, every single person you're ever in contact with (past, present, and future) will not receive eternal salvation, and it will be all your fault. You're taking everyone to Hell with you, and that's so much worse. Don't be selfish!"

When people are put in this type of cage, it's impossible to see through a window of open-mindedness, let alone hold faith in any sort of real present life, past lives, other people, spirituality, or the love that exists.

Since these vibrations came from people outside of our religion, they were considered foreign entities and weren't welcome in our households' soul space. Presence, past life understandings, and so much more were not of our faith, and therefore, wouldn't be with our religion. Riding through this fire wounds the child's heart. The true family I felt most connected to, my blood family that truly loved us, wasn't good enough by certain standards and was therefore banned because of one-sided religious beliefs. I was forced to abide in a tribe full-time that felt completely foreign to me.

Tapping into mechanisms for salvation as a young child, such as empathy or an open mind and heart, was all against the rules. When domesticated beliefs become our thoughts and feelings, the sense of deep responsibilities and our core beliefs take their toll emotionally, mentally, spiritually, and physically, to the point of death. This place of the first death is also the same place where we may begin to see the possibility of having a one-on-one relationship with Source, our Creator. This space is where the clues on what should be done next live.

Aligning with an open mind and an open heart is part of it—allowing the personal relationship with God to play out without interruption from any egoistic outside forces. Caged thoughts and feelings from these outside forces certainly bring unhappiness to all animals. Finding gratitude within the cocoon will break the seal on this cage that many of us are or were trapped inside. The more things we can possibly be grateful for, the sooner the doors of freedom will burst open and disintegrate into nothing.

Early on, I learned to survive on gratitude. Despite the heavy curse I carried on this tiny little girl's shoulders, I felt privileged to be raised on a working ranch. Ranch-related chores, church meetings, studying, and public school consumed my time. I worked even harder to realize the ecstasy of the moment of the freedom to ride. Exploring with our ranch horses deep in the forest helped me lose myself in the semblance of a perceived childhood.

At one point, a family friend gave me her beloved horse. She was a jet-black thoroughbred, which was the first big animal medicine presented to me. My horse journey began as Atman came in the form of my adopted mother (who was not affiliated with our church), passing down her ways to me. Being surrounded by four older brothers who taught me the cowboy ways did not leave much room for the tenderness of the feminine. I was gifted with the much-needed soft hands for my new gorgeous and perfect horse, balancing the masculine and feminine. She gave me the gift of true horsemanship that surpassed what most were accustomed to, truly saving my life.

I never dismounted and went on professionally training countless horses for the next 35 years. Every day and every night, I was on horseback looking for moments of bliss. There is a special place of firmness yet surrendering to humility when you're on horseback. With lots of love and time put into training, reaching a neutral point with this amazing spirit, partnered up, taps into Heaven in many ways. It's a very desirable place to be. This is the only thing on Earth that kept me here.

I rode through the fire of suicide, internal heartbreak, and the renunciation of parents with an entire known tribe as I left the church and the only belief system I knew, jumping out of one frying pan into another, experiencing years of trauma with no support. I now see how important all of this was as part of my tiger journey, consistently on the hunt for truth. I hunted for a way to see the universe shift what was out of my control.

Riding wild horses, I left the toxic safety of the church, entering another hell. Working with soul contracts, sorrow, and pain, I embarked on a 20-year partnership of sweat, blood, dirt, and broken bones. The new tribe I was surrounded by excelled in textbook narcissism, mixed with narcotic and alcohol abuse. During this time, I rode through the fire of the cocoon, spiritually awakening through a broken neck and jaw injuries. While I now live in 'aliveness,' I still have lifelong chronic syndromes because of these events. Out of a grave that came with this first death, I saw that I must evolve or repeat the past. Identifying the pain body, it was time to heal my broken bones and process the things I'd been spiritually downloading. Being still and gaining inner power, yet physically healing through multiple surgeries, caused me to come out as an even stronger warrior. Dragonfly enters my everyday life to hold me close as an angel, bringing me patience and stillness, along with toughness, since they've existed for over 3,000 years. Dragonfly teaches me (again) to balance the masculine and feminine parts of my character.

At this time, digging deep into the way of the Toltec, which is certainly the medicine to be seeking for anyone with caged thoughts, I came across the simplicity of their explanation of Heaven on Earth and how it's accessible to us personally at any time during our lifetime. I knew from personal experience we were living in Hell. Yet this way allowed me to explore as if I could see the magic switch within my reach, using gratitude as the tool to flip it in search of Heaven on Earth during this lifetime.

Riding through this new fire, I was determined to heal myself, cut all cords with toxic and unhealthy baggage, dedicate myself to the Creator, and experience what we speak of. Breaking away from my career and the only thing I knew, unable to physically ride horses again, I set out in search of what Source would provide.

Through acceptance, things began to shift, and I saw what I deserved for all of my pure faith and hard work. I would manifest and create my own life from here on, consistently encouraging transition into my higher self, balancing the masculine and feminine I carry, and using gratitude as my main life tool. I would be thankful for every possible thing I saw rather than the negative illusion of the circumstances. I thirsted to create the life I felt would get me further down the enlightened road.

Before I knew it, just like a light switch, Heaven appeared within me day after day as I literally packed up my horses, work dogs, and child, taking off into the wilderness where we'd heal. I'm a pure cowboy, so I'd never imagined a 'knight in shining armor.' Once I healed myself, my twin flame came fast as a shaman buckaroo, healing me in every way left possible. Together, we created Heaven on Earth daily in true form.

The Medicine

Finding your own medicine may have already come, or you may feel like that concept is far away. Your medicine is a gift for the betterment of humanity, and it makes your soul shine, plain and simple. That is what the saying means when referring to 'your life's purpose.' If you know what is for you, ride for it like no other! Every speed bump is worth all of the effort to live your life in a heavenly state. If you're too exhausted for now, receive and gather what works for you in your personal basket of tools to get through your awakening. Maybe someday you will share it. Ride through the fire and you'll gain strength.

When you're at your best, express gratitude. When you're at your worst, express gratitude. Thankfulness in any form will shift the vibrations of your circumstances to what's best for your highest good.

I remember waking up from my neck surgery, unable to move any muscle in my entire body because it was on lockdown. I started by counting the holes in the tile of the hospital ceiling, thankful that my voice box was okay. Gratefulness will always work as a personal shovel if you're in any sort of hole. Continuing this practice at all times is part of your medicine. How far you take this medicine of gratitude is how much you'll be grateful for. It'll bring awareness to your life, and with that, we learn to balance the masculine and feminine in a way that serves our highest good.

Accepting help from the outside can be a good idea when presented in alignment with your journey, filling your soul with peace and happiness.

The tribe you can trust from outside of your cocoon are people with no ego. You'll have to ride through some fire, but they will safely hold space for your path of self-healing in search of your Heaven on Earth.

Chakra healing will ignite other important resources for your medicine basket. Reaching out to angels and your animal guides who come to us in forms we can accept, relying on their messages to show you the way that's best for your path.

My adopted mother and I met on the battlefield three years ago, when she summoned me to administer her death with dignity juice into her hands. Another fire to ride through! We were now full circle. She saved my life, and I saved hers. I've been rewarded fully. Today, I live with Black Jaguar Medicine, soaking up what I can from what it has to offer. I've received clarity that solitude and observation are key forms of medicine for my survival right now. Breathwork Ceremony has opened all of the doors with the answers I've ever searched for. I spend quality time with her as 'Atman,' the most beautiful white horse with a black mane and tail. I've been searching for this white horse around every waking corner for the last eight years since a shaman expressed that I would "See it as a sign of my confirmation." She comes to me with healing, clarity, and messages, guiding me on how to open my heart and be love. She and this Jaguar race down the coastline of the jungle, neck and neck in my journey, although she laughs at the idea of me ever winning. Most of my healing tools, such as rattle and drum, are made from horsehide to facilitate my clients' journeys.

Once you've healed yourself and have raised the bar on who has access to your energy, you may also find yourself in a place to heal others in some ways from your basket. Turning hurt into compassion is the highest form of magic in human form. It sounds easy, but it's a ride through fire. Just like me writing this chapter for others, I hope your hurt can transform into compassion somehow as well.

MY LOVE LETTER TO YOU

"I am grateful that you've opened yourself up and are searching for what your soul seeks. Be aware that it takes time to process and heal. My prayer for you is that you just don't hold back! Don't let anyone manipulate and force their spiritual beliefs, or even simple things such as what you should eat for dinner, onto you. You are here with your own identity and God-given intuitions. Own them and be proud of what your Creator has given you, remembering your birthright of free will. With time so valuable, stop sitting in anything not meant for you. Shine your bright light. It's actually a lot easier than you think!

I'll be here for you in your time of need, riding through fire. Speeding towards the day we rejoice, riding even harder and faster through the High Sierra meadows, full of blue forget-me-not flowers, with our arms straight out to our sides and our heads thrown back in the wind, in Heaven on Earth, here and now. I'll now be packing our picnic lunch in a saddlebag for us to share out there. It must be created!"

As a lifelong rancher and professional horse trainer living day-to-day with chronic repercussions from serious injuries, April reached out to alternative medicine in search of living a pain-free and natural lifestyle. Feeling the call to help others experience the same opportunities, Buckaroo Buddha Holistic Healing LLC was established in 2019 by April and Dustin Kaiser. Building a Bridge for the ranching community and those alike, providing physical, mental, and spiritual well-being. Peace, health, and cowboy shit.

- Bowen Therapy Specialist

- Reiki Energy Healing and Ceremony

- Shamanic Practitioner

- Buckaroo Buddha Breathwork Facilitator

- Member of Brave Badass Healers Community - working closely with religious trauma and your spiritual awakening, narcissism abuse support, cord cutting, and removing attachments. She shares her authentic journey, cowboy logic, and straightforwardness, creating a path aligned with your soul's journey and highest good.

Connect with April Kaiser:

Email: buckaroobuddha1111@gmail.com

Website: https://www.buckaroobuddha.com

LinkedIn: https://www.linkedin.com/in/buckaroo-buddha-4137a2232/

Facebook: https://www.facebook.com/buckaroobuddha1111

Instagram: https://www.instagram.com/buckaroobuddha1111/

GRATEFULNESS IS A MAGIC TOOL THAT WILL SHIFT
THE VIBRATIONS OF YOUR CIRCUMSTANCES TO WHAT'S BEST
FOR YOUR HIGHEST GOOD. IT CAN BE IN ANY FORM, BIG OR SMALL.
IT COMES FROM WITHIN YOUR TRUE SELF.

~ APRIL KAISER

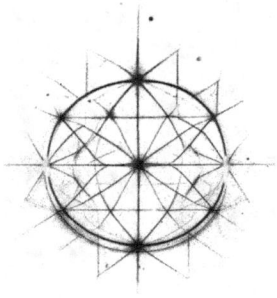

Chapter 17

HAWK EYES

The Awareness You Need to Lead
Laura Di Franco, MPT, Publisher

𝔐y 𝔖tory

"Oh shit!"

No one else was in the car, and no other cars were on the road when I swerved across the double yellow lines. The hawk came from the trees on my right and swooped down toward my windshield before flying off to the left.

The excellent reflexes from fourteen years of martial arts training came in handy. My body performs at peak levels, even for everyday moments like this. I was okay physically, but my mind had a field day.

Are you paying attention, Laura? You're on track. Let go. Surrender. Stop worrying. Was this sign good enough?

"Fuck you," I said out loud, trying to catch my breath. And then, I laughed for the next five minutes as I drove to class.

Just the day before, the request in my living room went something like, "Show me a sign I can't ignore."

My healer coaches say you can be a bit demanding with the Universe and your Spirit guides sometimes. I never felt like that was very respectful, but I guess one has to ask for what they want! I certainly needed some practice with that after a life of people-pleasing. Recovering good girl here. Anyone?

Dr. Stephen Farmer's *Animal Spirit Guides* is sitting on my side table. I use it almost every few days when the Spirit world talks to me in the form of animals. Hawks and other big birds have been signs for me for a long time. I'm not sure when that started.

I love birds, all of them. I always have. There's a feather tattooed on my left forearm with the initials YFIB (Your Fear Is Boring). I needed a post-divorce reminder. I wanted the birds and the reminder to be with me every day. The tattoo hurt like hell. I'm not one of those tattoo-addicted people. You won't see me with another one any time soon.

The reminder, though, is to go for the joy. I've been reminding myself for the last eight years, consistently, as a practice, in lots of different ways.

Joy is the ultimate sign I'm on track. The hawks help, and they show up a lot.

"Ah! Look up!"

I shouted to my sister as we walked, turning back toward her with some furious finger pointing, almost losing my hat in the process.

"Do you hear it? That's a hawk!" I craned my neck back to find it soaring in the middle of the bright blue winter sky. It called about ten times in a row.

"What do you think it's telling us?" My sister paused on the trail about ten paces behind me to look up.

"Everything is going to be okay. You're on track. You're on the right path," I said. "They've been around to give me that message for a while now."

I flash to myself in high school, in a stranger's bathroom at a party my friends brought me to. Staring in the mirror at my feathered hair, I leaned over the counter and sniffed up a line of coke. The boyfriend's brother was a drug dealer, and I was a very insecure, introverted loner. The drugs helped me lose my inhibitions, until they got in the way of my soccer career. Thank God the peak performer in me overpowered the not-good-enough part. I'm grateful for my drive and ambition as an athlete every single day. If it weren't for my body awareness and my love of what's possible, I'm not sure where I'd be today.

You've come a long way from that day, the voice whispers.

Everything you've been through has helped you become who you are now. It's okay. It's time to let go of the shame. It's even time to let go of the drive to push your body to the limit. It's okay to slow down.

Not yet, I thought in reply.

My sister and I continue to hike along the trail, deep in conversation about our lives, where we've been, and what's happening now. "We have good genes," she says. We're interested in the DNA that created our high-achieving bodies. Each of us has been a marathoner, and she, an experienced yogi; I, a third-degree black belt. Being in our bodies has been the foundation of the awareness and the secret behind mastering the language of our souls.

Deep awareness has always been a gift between my sister and me. And deeper conversations, connection, and understanding, even when we were living 5000 miles apart, were always present. Now that we're living five miles from each other for the first time in almost 30 years, I struggle with my awareness practice.

What's wrong with you? Why do you feel so uncomfortable?

I think this, but already know why. I'm asking myself the questions I'm afraid to answer.

Your fear is boring, I hear.

"Fuck you!" I say to that wise voice, again laughing out loud. Don't you love that Source has a wicked sense of humor?

The problem with tattooing something on your body that stands for something is that the reminder pops up, even when you don't want it to.

The awareness I've practiced in the last decade of my life means a lot of things to me. It's a survival mechanism, a business coach, a relationship counselor, and above all, a deep knowing and inner wisdom I now trust more than most people I know. There's nothing wrong with people. It's just that no other person will ever know what's aligned for me, so I've learned to take people with a grain of salt. In some cases, I take them with the whole container.

Whether that awareness comes in the form of a hawk, other animals, flickering lights, repeating numbers, the a-ha in someone's words, or the download moving through me to the page, my channel is open, and I don't plan on closing it again. But on this day, I'm thinking: *I'm ready to move to the Caribbean and sell coconuts. I'm done.*

With awareness, we have a choice.

And with awareness, sometimes the choices are painful. Today I feel the world conspiring against me in so many ways, making me afraid, again, to take the risks I know will catapult me toward my dreams.

What do you want, Laura?

I like that question, but I'm tired.

I thought I figured that out already, I plead in reply.

Recent circumstances are creating self-doubt and confusion.

You know the self-doubt and confusion are a "no;" you teach people this!

The wise voice is annoying me. Annoyance, I've learned, is a form of resistance in me. I recognize this as one of the signs, the secret internal language I pay attention to.

I choose to leave this one for the next life, I think. *I'm tired. I'm done,* I repeat.

I've learned to observe myself and my life like a hawk. I've learned to take that birds-eye view, soar higher, and take in a bigger picture. I've learned to be aware that I don't know the whole big picture most days and to trust there is one.

I've learned that to help others (anyone), you must model a certain level of awareness. These ninja moves of mindset and awareness help me lead others to their own wisdom. It's my practice of awareness that makes me a leader. And that's the reason I can't give up.

I want to be that leader. I don't want to give up. I talk with the wise me and tell her I'm in it for the long haul. But I do ask for a vacation.

It might be a conversation I don't want to have, or brave words I want to share (in a good way, like saying "I love you") that scare me. It could be a request that feels bold, or saying a sacred "no" to maintain boundaries that keep me healthy. In any of the ways I start to feel that feeling, I know that. If I don't address it, the Universe will continue to bring it to the forefront of my life until I pay attention and deal with it.

Sometimes she sends hawks to my windshield. "Fuck you, Universe!"

Okay, well, maybe not "Fuck you," but seriously, haven't I done enough this round?

Do you all know the saying they tell you when things suck that goes something like: "God won't give you anything you can't handle?" I call BS on that. There are a lot of circumstances in life that people don't handle well or can't handle at all. There are so many things I've been through that showed me what I was made of, and also events that showed me where I fall short. Some days, I'm happy to have just survived the moments without killing anyone or giving up.

Why is life so easy? Why is everything turning out for the best?

The *why* questions were a little tool I picked up from Dr. Noah St. John's book, *Millionaire Afformations.* He turned "affirmations" into "afformations" by putting the statements into question form because our brains are wired to solve problems. When I first started writing, recording, and listening to them, I felt goosebumps. The difference between making statements I half believed (affirmations) and asking questions (afformations) was palpable. I felt the shift like when the final puzzle piece slides effortlessly into its place with a touch of one finger.

Why is this resistance in me about talking to my family about the discomfort I feel being around them dissolving so easily?

I taste the feeling inside. I like it. It's not too bitter. It's not difficult. So, I try it again, slightly differently.

Why is this feeling of dread about talking to my family disappearing as I speak?

I trust that my inner wisdom will sort it out. And as I write and speak these words and stare out the sliding glass doors at the patio, a tiny little fuzzy-headed grey puff-ball of a bird lands on the chair back, hops to the ground, makes another hop a foot closer to the window, and looks up at me for at least five seconds before hopping away.

Hey there, Laura; you got this. You're on the right track. I love you.

With a small, closed-lipped smile, I close my journal, filled with purpose, release the dread, and get on with something way more aligned: The joy.

I use writing as an awareness practice. It's my main medicine and modality of self-development, along with body awareness meditation practices that I use sitting, walking in the woods, in the bath, and at my desk. Writing is my main channel, and when I connect to my body, stay present, and allow myself to gently move from a ruminating mind to a neutral, more peaceful zone, the writing usually comes fast and furiously. Many times, poems come out. This one about self-love changed how I viewed my self-care practice as a leader.

HOW DEEP IS YOUR LOVE?

By Laura Di Franco

I think my love goes deep.
And when it seeps back to me
in rings of grit
staining my skin and soul,
I sit in wonder.

But, really, is it any wonder?
I think that love is for others first.
And sure,
loving them is very good,
but not quite as great
as the state of deep love
I shower on myself.

When I keep it running longer,
making others wonder
when I'll come out
and if I saved any for them
only then. . .
. . . only then is when I know
it's deep enough.

Because the deep love I give to me
is the roots of the tree
that feeds everything
and everybody else.
I will only grow as high
as those roots are deep.

So, today I plant the seed,
worship the sun
nourish myself with love,
give my roots enough time
to find their way to the core,
a place I'm sure
they'll never be unearthed.

Grounded, centered, and strong
in that place,
that love,
that knowing,
That solid foundation
is where it all begins.

Is today your beginning?
How deep is your love?

It's not about taking care of yourself. It's about how you love yourself, said the wise voice.

Get your food right, do the exercise, take the forest baths and the lavender essential oil ones too, but remember to love on yourself by always soaring high, staying aware, and loving yourself fiercely, first. You get to come first. It's okay.

So, just like how I used my body as the channel throughout my entire life as an athlete, whether it was on the soccer field, running marathons, or sparring with my opponents in Tae Kwon Do, I pause to connect today in that place that knows, my body-mind. I watch her like a hawk.

Today's sacred place is quieter. She can sit still much longer. And when I give myself permission to surrender, I lie back in it like an inner tube down the lazy river at The Bellagio. It's a free-flowing, sun-shining, pina-colada-sipping, glitter-sparkling, bask-in-the-joy kind of feeling.

I'd like to help you write your way there. That's the place you'll live, thrive, and lead from as you evolve into who you were born to be.

ᛏHE ᛗEᛞɪᴄɪɴE

WATCH YOURSELF LIKE A HAWK:
HOW TO USE WRITING AS AN AWARENESS TOOL

This whole chapter was channeled. It's being edited and proofed, but the rough draft happened within about 45 minutes, where I breathed first, cleared my mind, and got out of the way of the message meant to move through.

That is some writing badassery. I want you to get to know your connection at that level, too. I want you to trust that the message is there whenever you choose to connect. I call this Brave Story Medicine™.

What you need:

A timer

A notebook

A pen

STEP ONE: CONNECT TO YOUR BODY

Practice paying attention to your breath for five minutes. Set a timer, get comfy, and begin. Relax, soften, and release with each exhale. Breathe deeply into the pelvic bowl and expand your ribs out on all sides, front and back. Feel everything. Remember, you have feet. What do you notice in terms of sensations? Be curious. Observe by feeling. Do thoughts come? Observe your thinking without attaching to the thoughts. Don't allow a thought to distract you from the sensations in your body. If it does, bring yourself back. Practice this until the timer goes off.

STEP TWO: WRITE YOUR HEART AND SOUL OUT

Grab your pen and notebook and set a timer for five minutes. Fill in the blank: I feel. Write as fast as you can without censoring yourself. Don't worry about punctuation, grammar, or even finishing sentences. No rules;

just write. Allow the message moving through you to come through the pen to the paper.

STEP THREE: WRITE TO UNDERSTAND YOURSELF

Grab your pen and notebook and set a timer for five minutes. Fill in the blank: The resistance in me feels like _____. Write as fast as you can without censoring yourself. Don't worry about punctuation, grammar, or even finishing sentences. No rules; just write. Allow the message moving through you to come through the pen to the paper.

STEP FOUR: WRITE TO CLAIM YOUR DREAMS

Grab your pen and notebook and set a timer for five minutes. Fill in the blank: If there were no one left to offend, upset, or disappoint, I would _____. Write as fast as you can without censoring yourself. Don't worry about punctuation, grammar, or even finishing sentences. No rules; just write. Allow the message moving through you to come through the pen to the paper.

STEP FIVE: WRITE TO MANIFEST YOUR DREAMS

Grab your pen and notebook, and this time, take as much time as you need to reverse-journal the last bit of writing you did. Read the Step Four writing out loud to yourself. Then, write as if you're living your dream now. Start with this: I'm so happy and grateful now that _____.

No rules; just write. Allow the message moving through you to come through the pen to the paper.

Lastly, what are you feeling? What did the prompts bring up for you? Which felt good? Which felt some other way? Notice everything. Watch everything like a hawk. Notice what is there to teach you and what's there to help you help guide others to their inner wisdom.

BONUS STEP FOR MY LEADERS

Create a blog or social post from one of the prompts and share it. Your words change the world when you're brave enough to share them. Lead from joy. Lead from awareness. Lead from love.

Laura Di Franco, CEO of Brave Healer Productions, is an award-winning publisher specializing in business strategy for holistic health and wellness professionals ready to become bestselling authors. She has 30 years of expertise in holistic physical therapy, 14 years of training in martial arts, and her company has published over 100 Amazon bestselling books. The community is over 3000 authors strong, and the mission is to wake the world up to what's possible.

Laura is a spoken-word poet, inspirational speaker, and lover of dark chocolate. She has a contagious passion for helping you share brave words that build your business and leave your legacy. Want some advice about your book idea? Schedule a chat with our publishing team!

Connect with Laura:

Website: https://lauradifranco.com

Facebook: https://www.Facebook.com/BraveHealerbyLaura/

Instagram: https://www.Instagram.com/BraveHealerProductions

Linked In: https://www.linkedin.com/in/thelauradifranco/

YouTube:
https://www.youtube.com/c/BraveHealerProductionswithLauraDiFranco

WITH AWARENESS, YOU HAVE A CHOICE. CHOOSE LOVE.

~LAURA DI FRANCO

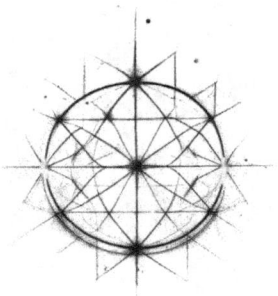

Chapter 18

MASSAGING THE HEART OF MY SOUL

From Teenage Motherhood to the Healing Path

Sharla Duncan

My Story

My daughter's body was trapped, just as my soul felt trapped. We were mirrors—her stiff muscles, my frozen spirit.

I was 17 when life cracked me open. A child myself, I carried my first daughter into this world. Her father, just 19, wasn't ready. The pressure broke him, and he buried himself in work, leaving me alone to carry what felt unbearable. I slipped into the shadows of postpartum depression, gaslit by doctors and dismissed by a culture with no language for my pain.

I took a year away from school to give her life, then returned a married girl with a baby. The halls that once held my laughter now echoed with whispers and bullying. I was a wife, mother, and a teenager with a disabled child the world refused to name.

At 18, I sat alone in a doctor's office, grappling with the words *cerebral palsy*. Back then, all I received was a thin paragraph in a medical book, a sentence in an encyclopedia. A name without a map. Still, I did what any mother would do: I loved her as if she were whole.

When her body cramped and she cried, my heart wrenched.

Is this my fault?

I quickly regained composure, remembering my grandmother and mother's hands. I massaged her tiny limbs, and in those moments, she softened, as if my touch was the only doorway into peace. For months, she barely slept, yet when I pressed my palms and fingertips into her tiny body, she quieted.

In healing her, I began to unknowingly heal myself. And then, just like that, I divorced at 21. Left to rebuild my shattered heart once again, I searched for something, anything, to reach into my soul and massage the fragments of love that remained.

At 22, life stirred within me once again. Another daughter blossomed in my womb, a reminder that life always moves forward, this time by choice. The innocence in her tiny smile, the sunlight in her wide, sunflower eyes, spilled joy into the hollow places of my soul. Yet the bond that brought her into this world wasn't love; it was born from a tether of pain, a relationship forged in the fire of trauma rather than the warmth of true connection.

Years later, in a season of searching, the medicine of Raynor Massage found me.

A coupon. A question. *Who even gives two hours of massage?*

But when I finally received it, my heart cracked wide. This wasn't just massage; it was soul work.

I practiced gratitude with *The Magic* by Rhonda Byrne at the time, and on one of those days, I gathered every coin I ever saved—loonies, toonies, and old dollar bills in a container full of tips from my hairstyling days that was lost in a moving box for a decade. When I poured it out, I wept. It was exactly what I needed to make the down payment for my training to begin.

That was the moment Spirit showed me: The Universe conspires when you dare to walk your medicine path. What began as survival became initiation. What began as depression became devotion. What began as a mother's desperate search became the foundation of a healer's life.

And there, in the upper corner of the room, I witnessed myself receiving a massage.

What's happening?
Where am I?
Am I dead?

There I lay face down. This gentleman stood by my head, pressing his elbow into my back. "Breathe with me."

My body surrendered with a deep inhale and an unrestricted exhale—a sigh of release, if I may. Our breathing fell in sync. As he approached my mid-back, he held a spot that seemed so intense. I couldn't breathe, yet I could. I wanted to fight back.

*But this **is** what I desired.*

This was exactly what I yearned for all those years. He held space for the expansion, as if reaching in past my ribcage, knowing exactly what I needed, as if our souls conversed. This level of communication was unfamiliar.

He held the intense ache in my heart, allowing me to feel genuine love and care: a conflict due to the heartfelt pain through my chest. I cycled between sobbing, laughing, and screaming.

He encouraged *all* that; he allowed me to express the way I needed.

I didn't get shushed.
I wasn't told it was wrong.
He didn't tell me to stop!

He just held space. He allowed me to breathe through the intensity of that deep-rooted agony within me. *Is he massaging my heart? How can this be?*

Then came the drumming.
The drumming was so intense.
It was so loud, so rhythmic, (sigh) so soothing.

I was terrified, yet I felt peace and serenity.
I was confused yet elated.

There was such a deep, agonizing pain, yet a complete sense of freedom within my body. As I watched him, I realized something—his touch was so gentle, yet somehow, he guided me exactly where I needed to go. It clicked for me in that moment: *The magic isn't just in what he's doing, but in the space he's holding for me. He's giving me room to do the work I didn't even know waited inside me.* My spirit recognized it instantly, because I spoke of that very thing so many times before—it was exactly what I longed for.

A modality that could **reach into my soul and massage my heart.**

He turned me over, so I was face-up, and asked permission to work in my belly. As soon as he began, vivid visuals appeared, the drumbeat syncing perfectly with my heartbeat. I felt completely safe wrapped in comfort, and in that deep sense of safety, I lost all awareness that I was receiving a massage.

Everything vibrated, and I didn't know what was happening. I continued to breathe deeply. I slipped out of my body again.

The vibration is so strong.

Waves rushed down to my feet, then rose back up to my heart, repeating again and again. I felt his hands move to my head. He gently massaged my temples. My breathing started to slow. The vibrations settled.

I heard him say, "Thank you for letting me work on you today."

His energy detached from mine. I still floated, but this time, I was tethered—like a helium balloon tied to a chair. He left the room, and the massage was over, but I was completely unaware of it.

I heard and felt the voices of generations of women before me, their cries mingling with whispers of gratitude, thanking me for doing this work for them. I didn't even know what work I did—all I knew was I surrendered, drifting deeper, simply allowing myself to feel.

A sudden knock at the door—a female voice asking, "Are you okay?" —and just like that, *thump!* I was back in my body.

"Yes, I'll be right out."

I'm anchored with a new awareness.

Apparently, I fell asleep or went into a dream state for 30 minutes after the massage ended.

I came out of the room and sat down at the table with the practitioner to collect myself. My mind was blown.

"So, I'm not sure what just happened, but I want to thank you for reaching into my soul and massaging my heart."

He grinned and said, "You're welcome."

"How much is it to take the course?" I inquired.

"You get a discount for receiving a massage beforehand. The value you paid online will be taken off the course."

"Do you take cash?"

"For all of it?" He snickered. "Who carries that amount of cash around?"

"I was taking it to get a bank draft to apply for the RMT course, but I feel called to learn this style."

I went out to my vehicle, got my containers, and paid him in cash.

Now that I've shared the profound impact Raynor Massage had on my life, I want to share a simple technique with you.

✟ʜᴇ ᴍᴇᴅɪᴄɪɴᴇ

What is Raynor Massage? Raynor Massage is not Registered Massage Therapy.

Australian-trained natural path Brandon Raynor developed this system of bodywork that encompasses both the muscular and the skeletal systems of the body.

Each person is treated as a holistic organism while considering the inner complexity of needs and the entire body. Each person is unique, so their assessment and treatment should be as well.

My main goal is to seek out residual body tightness and blockages and remove them. I accomplish this in part through various Eastern forms of massage, such as Shiatsu massage, Ayurvedic massage, Eastern chiropractic work, Lomi-Lomi, and breathwork.

I also apply Eastern medical theories that focus on freeing disruptions in the body's life force, emotions, and subtle energies, often referred to as chi, qi, or Prana. We do this through what we call Bands of Tension.

As a Raynor massage specialist, my purpose is to utilize any number of techniques and practices catering to each individual's specific needs.

In my practice, I like to start the massage by connecting with my person, in the form of coaching the breath, so we become synced. Rocking the body to release any surface tension, like the way a dog shakes off the excess water from its body, allows us to assist the person to break through the initial energetic armor and start to relax and sink into not only the table, but the experience.

We hold residual tension in our feet and hands, and those body parts so often get neglected. I like to take time to assess the feet and feel what type of tension they hold.

Our big toe tension travels all the way to the tip of the head. A powerful way to release tension in your entire body is to release the big toe.

- On either side of the nail bed, but not directly on, gently squeeze and rotate back and forth. I'm looking for tension that could feel like a tight thread or a grain of sand.

- When you find it, bring a scale into your mind (one to ten), with ten being the maximum amount of pressure you can take. Hold that spot with the pressure of about a seven or an eight and breathe into it until it lowers to a four. Don't move on to your next spot until it releases.

- When it releases, continue to feel and palpate the area until you find another spot that has a tight thread and repeat the process.

- Do this procedure with each toe, starting at the tip, feeling free to pull the knuckle if it feels stuck.

- When you're done, you can shake your foot to move the energy and move to the other foot.

- You can also use this same procedure on your hands.

- Or better yet, get someone else to do it for you!

It's an honor to share my journey with you. I'd love to connect if you'd like to learn more about Raynor Massage or the other medicine I house.

Sharla Duncan's journey as a wellness practitioner began with motherhood at the age of 17.

At a young age, she gave birth to two daughters who faced significant health challenges from the start. Her eldest was born with cerebral palsy, and her youngest with jaundice. Both had severe childhood allergies.

Determined to find answers beyond the limitations of conventional medicine, Sharla set out to explore natural and holistic approaches. That search not only brought healing support for her children but also opened the door to her own profound path of self-healing, growth, and discovery.

In June 2012, Sharla experienced her first Raynor Massage session with Terry Masson. The two-hour treatment left such an impact, she knew instantly she found something extraordinary. By September, she completed her training.

The following year, she advanced her training with Brandon Raynor himself, deepening her skill and expanding her dedication to this powerful modality.

In 2016, Sharla established *Just Breathe Massage* in Kelowna, B.C.

Her commitment and passion led her to become an Instructor of Raynor Naturopathic Massage in February 2019, an honor that allows her to train practitioners and share the depth of this modality with others on their own healing journeys.

Sharla enriches her practice through a wide spectrum of modalities, including Body Talk (Modules 1 & 2), Mindscape, Break Through, Free Fall, Swedish massage, European lymph drainage, Reiki (Master level), and Energy Balancing. Each layer of training enhances her ability to hold space for holistic healing, but her foundation remains rooted in the belief that body, mind, and spirit are inseparably connected.

Today, Sharla Duncan continues to walk this path as a practitioner, teacher, and guide, devoted to helping others breathe deeper, heal fully, and rediscover their wholeness.

Connect with Sharla:

Website: https://justbreathewellness.ca

Instagram: https://www.instagram.com/sharla.duncan.74/

Facebook: https://www.facebook.com/sharla.duncan.74

UNPLUG YOUR MIND, RECHARGE YOUR SOUL

~ UNKNOWN

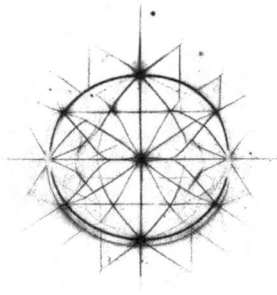

Chapter 19

HEALING DESPITE THEM

The Fine Balance Between Fuck You and Thank You
Angel Gold

𝕸𝔂 𝕾𝖙𝖔𝖗𝖞

It starts within
It is an internal game.
My own warrior stands watch.
I surrender to my warrior within.
I surrender to that part of me
that knows how to hold.
I lay my head in his lap.
Knowing I am held.
I am loved.
I am my own queen.
Curled up in my furry blankets,
allowing the cool breeze to caress my face.
The cosmos humming the tune of the great Mother.
As I lull myself to sleep, I dream of love.
Dream the sparkliest dream!
Your unique ray of light
deserves to shine from the heavens.

Permeating life and dancing with the stars,
holding hands with the love of your life within,
I allow myself to surrender and be held.
By the warrior within.

"You are not special!" she yells at me.

Laser beams shoot out of her eyes into my shattered heart as her poison drips into my cells. I recoil from the blast of her energy as it leaks and sinks into the corner where my inner child is hiding. I bring my full attention and protection to that space upon recovery, but it's too late. That arrow was a direct hit into my inner child's heart.

I gasp for air, physically convulsing like the computer inside my brain has just been reset. My nostrils flare with the fierceness of my warrior as I meet her glare with matched intensity. *Who the fuck do you think you are?* I glare wordlessly into the depths of her soul.

That was the beginning of the end of my relationship with that teacher.

I say beginning. Those of us who've struggled with being in a relationship with humans who choose subjugation over empowerment will understand. It takes a great amount of energy to leave abusive relationships, especially when you've been programmed to give your power away to that person.

Yes, they program us.

The skilled ones blanket their manipulation with the phrase, "Always give credit to your teacher," over and over. "Make sure you say where the information comes from when you start teaching." Yes. We learn that in school, right? References are a thing.

But when you find yourself saying, "So and so says this," every second sentence, it's time to bring awareness to how deeply you're being programmed.

There is a balance between honoring the teachings that are passed down and giving your power away to the teachings.

Mastery is formed by embodying and integrating the information, owning and birthing your own language, and the way to share teachings or your own medicinal art. It's formed with critical thinking and discernment about what serves you and what parts need to be let go of or transformed. You create internal knowledge within. You choose when you no longer need to reference every thought in your head.

It's part of the evolutionary process of humanity and the art of the sacred rebel.

Aligned and authentic teachers will allow you to go through this process and cheerlead you along your way. You'll find out quickly if the teacher you're working with is aligned with these principles by asking questions and reflecting upon their responses. In my experience with this teacher, I was sharing a mind-blowing experience that had me questioning my sanity, and I was asking for help.

What I did not know at that moment

was that I dove into a realm she had no access to.

She chose annihilation at that moment.

But heaven forbid I be an outcast from the community I had finally found. *Now what do I do? Shrink myself?* I have shared all my darkest secrets with these humans, and we are all now trauma-bonded to the one in control.

I stayed, against my inner knowing. I stayed, knowing this circle was toxic.

I rationalized with myself: *This is part of the work; this is what we have been taught. Allow yourself to be triggered constantly in these circles so you can bring the traumas to the light and heal them.*

I found myself on my knees one night, rubbing cream into her thighs as she stood silent, and I thought: *What has happened to me? What the fuck am I doing right now?*

I learned the hard way that certain humans will take advantage of your gifts and siphon your energy from your heart if you let them.

Hear that again, fixer-pleasers.

Humans will take advantage of you as long as you let them.

For most humans, this is unconscious. They're just going along with their storyline, trying to survive. When they teach awareness and spirituality, there is a knowing.

When someone consciously takes advantage of you, there are many words that humans have creatively produced to label such dark magic and subjugation, and for these humans, boundaries and no contact become essential.

This, too, was another hard lesson taught to me by the same teacher. I was so entwined within this community, my want to be a part of the unit caused me to abandon myself, go against my inner intuition, and I allowed one of her assistants to take pictures of me, ending with skin and lace booty shorts.

Hundreds of pictures were captured of me running through the woods, playing as she encouraged me to take off more clothes. This was a very empowering experience, where I allowed myself to be seen in ways I've never done before, while several women cheered me on.

Quickly, the dark magic rolled in. "I am jealous of you," rolled off her venomous lips to my jaw-dropped face. Spells dropped as she whispered how often she gazed at my beautiful body for months, yet refused to give me the images.

The high priestess holding the container sides with my perpetrator, and I release myself from the circle.

Yet, I still was not done. I still didn't have enough energy to maintain the boundaries, as all my assault traumas resurfaced during this ordeal, and I found myself flailing with no support and spiraling into a mental breakdown. I found myself apologizing to my perpetrator as my energy dropped further and further. I grasped at any support I could find. I had released all my outside friends. All I had was this small circle of humans in my world. Enter my abandonment wounds.

Yes. The shadow work that emerged through the fires of this experience was epic!

Today, I can sniff a perpetrator miles away.

Fuck you.

Your energy is not welcome here.

And thank you.

Go ahead and share these beautiful pictures of the goddess with the world.

I dare you.

I have no shame. I have no fear.

Those pictures can only serve to empower me further.

Thank you, and fuck you can go together. It's spiritually balanced. I was taught by powerful shamans that all is energy; it's all perception. Some gold came out of this experience. If you think about how you feel when you're in love, your heart pounds, your heart rate increases, and your palms sweat. When you're in fear, your heart pounds, your heart rate increases, and your palms sweat. It's all perception around labeling the emotions racing through your soul basket.

Both can be true as you hold love in one hand and fear in the other.

When an experience like this happens, it takes time to unravel the traumas and energy lines this attaches to. It takes even longer when there is no accountability taken on the other end. When I did reach out to apologize, I was met with, "I was really hurt and this has had far-reaching effects, and I don't trust you." That was the final piece that allowed me to release myself from the toxic prison I had created.

I say, "I created," because nobody made me stay there. I had to take radical responsibility for the situation I got myself into and the humans I allowed within my inner circle. I allowed these humans to treat me this way in the name of healing.

I witnessed myself protecting my teacher, still giving her credit for all my knowledge, and hearing other teachers credit her for my gifts as I facilitated energy work on them. "Oh, she has really taught you well!"

Um, no. I came to her with those gifts, mastered already. Yet I said nothing.

As I stalk energy lines back into my past to find where else I had done that, of course, it made sense. I made excuses and hid the shadow aspects of my marriage for years, covering the abuse I endured, and putting on the white picket fence facade. Here it was showing up again.

Do not gossip about your teacher. Do not share about your circle sisters. You will cause drama. You will be kicked out of the whole community if you tell people what happens in these circles. Nobody will believe you. You are just looking for attention. Remember when so and so spoke out and she got excommunicated?

Grounding into Mother Earth, my roots wrapped around the fiery ball at the center of our planet, I hear the whisperings of Mama Gaia,

Remember, love, these were the people that put these dark spells on you:

You are not a writer.

The world is not ready for your gifts.

Your words will not be published in our community.

A small smile creeps across my face as I stand tall, roll my shoulders back, and feel the attachment of my crystalline wings, flutter and stretch to fill the room in full expansion.

Fuck you. And thank you.

Thank you for reminding me to go within, remember who I am,

the energy I house,

And what energy I will never allow into my world again.

I love you and I release you.

Hear me now. You are released.

And so it is.

There are gold and shadow aspects of all experiences.

The teachings revolve around re-authoring your story to serve you. For me, the gold of working with this woman brought me new teachings, traveling to novel places and having mind-blowing heart-expanding moments in time with myself and others within that circle.

I feel gratitude for the space held while I cleaned out divorce and abandonment wounds, the death of two partners, and a bacterial infection that almost killed me during this whole experience, which had me reeling.

The circle was there for me through it all.

Until I started healing. Heaven forbid we heal.

All was well until I started challenging the rules, asking questions, and stepping out of the Guru narrative that was programmed within us all. The addiction to suffering was kept alive as the dark energies were permitted to enter the sacred space and dance freely among us.

She did make it clear she struggled with boundaries herself. Another juicy nugget of wisdom drops in clearer.

If someone tells you they struggle with boundaries, believe them.

It's one thing to guess, based on their actions, and it's a whole other ballgame when they're up front with their weakness, and you still choose to step in.

Taking radical responsibility for your actions is where the healing begins.

Yes.

I did not listen to my intuition.

I abandoned myself.

I left my inner child unattended.

My warrior left his post.

Challenging her authority, not accepting her coaching style, and speaking my truth about the damaging effects of telling someone they are "not special" brought on a response that shifted me into another dimension.

"I am not your coach; I am your teacher."

I fired the teacher within myself. I put Willow White Wolf in a cage. The programming was so deeply ingrained, I became fearful of repeating my teacher's behaviors as I saw the same addiction to suffering showing up in my circles as I followed her rigid outline of how to run retreats and circles.

It took me years to come back to my own inner coach, the coach who raised hundreds of kids in the gym and preschool. The coach, who adored her babies, lifted them up and gave them a safe space to shine and grow.

That coach opened Willow White Wolf's den and brought in other expert teachers to heal my inner child and the wolf within.

Healing happens in layers. Honoring exactly where you are in your healing process is important. Sometimes you need to dive right into your rage and hold its hand for the fire to simmer. Sometimes you need to scream "fuck you" into the fire, to help you move through to the other side. Sometimes you can say "thank you" with respect and gratitude and walk away.

Knowing when to leave, honoring your intuition, and disconnecting will ultimately determine how much energy you need to put into healing yourself afterward.

The rage does dissipate over time.

And.

This is an important part of the process of letting go.

I choose not to live here.

I choose to go in, touch the wound, acknowledge what's there, apply the medicine, and come back up the root system. You don't have to live in the dark with it. Unhook. Come back to the sunshine and allow yourself to heal.

The Medicine

Sometimes deciding who you are is deciding who you will never be again.

My wish for you is to know love.

I want you to lean into the darkest parts of your soul, hold my hand, and walk through the Valley of Death, knowing you are safe.

Knowing the mystery of life becomes your friend when you hold its hand. The great mystery hums a tune you can match and sway with if you choose.

I want you to know the void; knowing this avatar I'm housed in allows you to touch the cosmos when you draft my energy.

My heart is right here; you're never alone, my love. Understand the gifts of your soul are waiting to be unearthed.

The cracks your heart has experienced allow the light to shine in and heal you from the inside out.

They shine like a prism of love, transforming your heart into the rays of the sun.

Allow the crack to open!

Stop trying to hold it all together. You must disassemble to reassemble. This is the cycle of life, my love.

Lean into the mother and allow yourself the rebirth you deserve. Yes, you can reincarnate on Earth in the same lifetime.

Say yes, give yourself permission, and allow your wounds to heal.

I have had the honor and privilege of sitting at the feet of many who called themselves 'teachers.'

I have learned a lot through the wisdom that they shared and the trauma I endured, both in my outside world and within theirs.

1. Always do your research on the humans you choose to allow into your inner world, especially if they're giving themselves labels such as teacher, guru, healer, leader, shaman, or elder.

2. Great marketing does not equate to a great teacher. Anyone can pay a professional to beat algorithms. Do not rely on the number of followers to determine your safety within a container.

3. Is this leader inclusive and open to questions that challenge their narrative?

4. Maintain boundaries as you engage and never dismiss your intuition. Use discernment when challenging your own agreements and ask for outside support if you are getting 'red lights' about an experience.

5. Are they saying you need them, or do you need the container they have provided?

6. Know your intent before entering. Do not get distracted by the sparkly 'side gigs.' Remember why you engaged in this community in the first place.

7. Remember, you are your greatest teacher. Do not give your power away and allow someone else to be your only guide.

THERE IS A BALANCE BETWEEN HONORING THE TEACHINGS
THAT HAVE BEEN PASSED DOWN AND GIVING YOUR POWER
AWAY TO THE TEACHINGS.

~ ANGEL GOLD

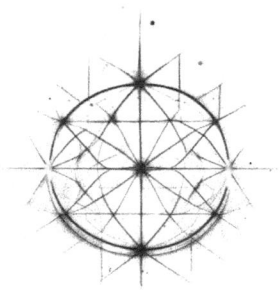

Chapter 20

SERVICE THROUGH LEADERSHIP

Leading From the Heart as Your New Way of Life
Angel Gold

As you step into service through leadership and choose to take on the responsibility of holding people's mental health in your hands, you need to understand the immense grounding and responsibility it takes when doing this kind of work.

**You can only teach and hold
to the level you're willing to teach and hold yourself.**

The following excerpt is from a student who was on the front line, in the trenches, and advocating for children's lives. The gratitude I have for these warriors of light, true, authentic healers, and champions of humanity is immense. This one has had a special place in my heart, and I'm honored to have been a part of their ascension process.

I know we were asked if we had done the "I see you" exercise, to say what we saw in the other person.

Where I struggled was when I saw some things that I did not want to say.

I know nothing is 'good or bad,' just the opposite, but we still label things that way.

When I looked at some people, I saw their heart, their wisdom, their warrior, their fire, but in others, I saw their longing for perfectionism, their immense guilt, huge pain, etc., and I was not comfortable speaking truthfully, what I saw or felt. I only wanted to see and say the 'good' things and was not sure how to say the harder ones, the darker ones, so I chose to say nothing at all.

What also stuck out is what you said, that when you see something in another, it is also a reflection of yourself, and that has stuck with me, which leads to today. I received an email from a mother who watched one of my presentations. This was a piece of it:

"I, too, went into postpartum psychosis after the birth of my second child. Unfortunately, my story ends in tragedy as I killed my youngest son four months after he was born. I thought my children were going to be kidnapped, raped, and tortured by an ex-boyfriend, and that this would continue for the rest of their lives. I am now trying to put my life back together, and I so desperately want to make up for what I did when I was sick."

I bawled. First, because of the incredible pain and heartbreak I feel.

But the second piece is because of the idea that what we see in others is a reflection of ourselves. The idea of separateness is simply an illusion of the ego, and we are not separate at all. It is easy to say 'I see you' or 'Namaste' in a yoga class or a room of like-minded people. Easier to see the similarity when we see the 'good,' the 'light,' and the 'nice.'

Where it is hard is when you see the 'dark,' 'bad,' 'ugly,' and 'hurt' in others and must acknowledge and accept those pieces within yourself and not play into the illusion of being separate.

I would like to think I am above killing my own son.

I would like to think she is psycho, and I was never crazy enough to do anything as horrific. But the truth is, I may have. My delusions were so incredibly real. I do not know that I would not have hurt or killed him. That is incredibly hard to sit with and uncover. To think that I may have done something to my own baby, to know I am not above that.

The only real difference I see between her and me is circumstance and privilege.

I had a family doctor who recognized my symptoms. My professional team knew me personally and had an incredible desire to support me in any way possible, and I had access to the best workers in the country to help me pull through, but she did not. The difference is, we simply have different lessons and journeys.

This leads to one of my deepest fears.

I know we can only push others as deep as we are willing to go as leaders. But I find the deeper I go and the more I realize we are not separate, the harder it is to work to truthfully accept myself and others, especially in those places that are difficult, if not completely disturbing.

The ones that are heartbreaking and gut-wrenching to get to and feel almost impossible to sit with, the places driven by fear, chaos, and deep pain.

The places or people I would so desperately want to pretend I was separate from and keep up the illusion, as sometimes the illusion is easier to take than the truth!

And part of me wants to just stay in the illusion, but I also believe in the polarity of the world.

To fully understand ourselves, we must explore the entirety of our own being.

To fully understand the infinite power of our own light, we must be brave enough to explore every crevice of our own darkness.

But to be honest, I am afraid of the dark.

*

Understand, this is the depths that I swim at and train at.

Gathering this constellation of authors and anchoring our mission to build warriors of light, as leaders of this new world, we are stepping into where leading by the heart is our way of life.

The authors I have gathered to write in this book have been vetted and are considered "safe containers" to do your work in. I only recommend healers I will go to myself, and here, I am introducing you to my care team.

There are many dabblers out there causing harm in our communities. I love that humans are waking up and starting to experiment; however, my mental health requires more than a recreational healer. We provide for you what we expect to be provided for us. If you choose us as your mirrors, we will expect you to meet us at the depths of your own soul.

The authors in this book met us and continue to "meet us" at that mysterious place that few choose to travel.

We encourage you to do your homework on who you choose to work with, and we encourage you to start with the authors in this book. The unique rays of light, the different languages, and the different tools all come from the same source place.

Ultimately, everything you need to achieve the level of consciousness you desire is already inside of you. You are the answer to your own question.

Do not look to others for the answers. Teachers and guides are there to assist you in remembering what you already know in your body and soul.

Look to those teachers who offer to help you find your own truth and not those who attempt to convince you of their truth. The ego will believe it is 'right' and everything else must be 'wrong.' Do not fall prey to this lie. Each ray of light has its own unique perspective.

We're all beings of infinite potential and unimaginable power. No one is above or below another. We are simply at different places on our journey to unlearn and remember our true selves.

The real work in this lifetime is to remember that you are love and connected to all of life. This connection brings with it all the knowing you seek and infinitely more. You must unlearn the misinformation that has been given to you, which has created this false sense of separation and limitation. It's only then that you can remember and reconnect with your true essence, your spirit.

You are perfect because you exist. All that exists is the creation of Source, the Universe, God, or whatever word you choose to represent this life force. All of creation is a beautiful expression of the perfection of life. Your perfection is not dependent on your current situation or circumstances.

Life is love, love is light, and light is all around and inside you. Each one of us is a unique ray of light emanating from the same Source of creation. When you remember that you are light, you regain the ability to shine this light on everything in your world. This is the power to co-create with life itself.

May you, too, follow your own unique ray of light and choose to shine bright for all the world to see.

YOU CAN ONLY TEACH AND HOLD TO THE LEVEL
YOU'RE WILLING TO TEACH AND HOLD YOURSELF.

~ANGEL GOLD

ABOUT THE AUTHOR

Angel Gold is a modern shaman, author, and visionary guide devoted to awakening sovereign leadership in a time of collective transformation.

Her journey has been one of fire, fracture, and rebirth. From surviving trauma and collapse to reclaiming her voice as a leader and medicine carrier, Angel embodies the path of the wounded healer who has transmuted her pain into power and created medicine for the world.

Her training has unfolded through years of direct apprenticeship and initiation with wisdom keepers across the Americas. She walked the dreaming path for over a decade with the **Toltec family of don Miguel Ruiz and don José Ruiz,** training in the Eagle Knight lineage of the Teotihuacan pyramids, Mexico.

She was initiated into **Andean and Incan medicine by Peruvian maestro Jorge Luis Delgado,** receiving teachings on crystal healing and the Chakaruna path of "bridge people." She sat in sacred plant ceremony, including with the first female Chief of the tribe, ayahuasquera in the Brazilian jungle, where she was recognized as carrying the spirit of Mama Ayahuasca from lifetimes before.

Each apprenticeship was not a certification on paper, but an initiation of the soul, lived, survived, and embodied.

These lineages continue to inform Angel's teachings, not as dogma but as living codes that she translates for a modern audience of leaders, seekers, and visionaries.

Her spiritual work blends Jaguar, Wolf, and Eagle medicine, Toltec wisdom, ancestral remembrance, and Fire Heart energy into a living system of shamanic leadership for today's world.

She then bridges that work with 30 years of training and healing high-performance athletes in multiple sports, including gymnastics, senior men's football, rugby, swimming, and NHL hockey.

Angel is the founder of *Nina Songo: The Fireheart Mystery School* and the creator of *Jaguar Wisdom: An Oracle of the Toltec Heart.*

She is also the international best-selling author of *Bytes of Light: Evolving Leadership for the Spiritual Entrepreneur* (under pen name Angel Rohrer) and the visionary behind multiple frameworks and offerings, including *The Horsehead Clause, The Boundary Queen* (sacred boundaries), and *Golden Mind, Fire Heart* (mental training and spiritual practice for athletes).

Her teachings remind us that leadership is not about hierarchy but about becoming a living ceremony—one who embodies courage, truth, and fierce compassion.

Through her writing, courses, and community, Angel teaches that stillness can be strength, rage can be holy, grief can hollow us into wisdom, and joy can be a radical act of sovereignty.

Her Fire Heart Mystery School gathers those ready to shed old agreements, reclaim their power, and rise as co-creators of a more sacred world.

When she is not teaching, Angel is a mother to both fur and humans, a dreamer, and a lifelong student of the wild and lover of dark chocolate.

The howl of wolves, the gaze of jaguar, and the whisper of wind through mountains are her daily teachers, reminding her that leadership is a dialogue with the more-than-human world as much as with people.

Connect with Angel:

Website: https://www.angelgold.ca/

Email: angel@angelgold.ca

Instagram: https://www.instagram.com/iam.angelgold/

Substack: Firelight and the Sacred Howl: https://substack.com/@angelgold

Fire Heart Mystery School Community:
https://www.skool.com/fire-heart-mystery-school

*

"My husband, Rob, and I spent the better part of five years working with Angel.

She is a true healer, very intuitive and creative in her treatments. She has been an integral part of my self-care when coping with anxiety, and I credit her with helping me get to a point where my anxiety has greatly decreased.

A huge success! She is stubborn and strong. She will find a way to release whatever you are holding on to through grounding, body awareness, energy, and crystal work. She is one of a kind; we highly recommend her!"

~ **Jessica Niedermayer, Singer/Songwriter, Wild Honey**
~ **Rob Niedermayer, NHL Hockey Hall of Fame**

*

"Angel Gold is pure magic wrapped in human form. She doesn't just talk about transformation, she *lives* it. Being around her feels like standing near a sacred fire that makes you see yourself more clearly and remember who you really are.

What I adore most about Angel and her work is how she bridges the mystical and the practical with such beauty and grace. She takes ancient wisdom and turns it into something that feels accessible, empowering, grounded, and real. Her work stirs up a part of you that's been dormant but now waiting to rise and shine again!

Through her FireHeart Mystery School, her books, and her powerful voice, Angel is redefining what it means to lead, to heal, and to love. She's fierce, grounded, deeply authentic, and a true modern-day medicine woman. I'm so grateful to walk beside her and witness the incredible ripple of light she's creating in the world."

~ **Shari Alyse, "America's Joy Magnet", Host & Executive Producer of "Good Morning Joy", 2x TEDx Speaker, Bestselling Author**

*

"Angie started coaching me in power tumbling and trampoline when I was about 11 years old. She immediately gave me so much support and encouragement to learn fast and get to higher levels for competitions. She believed in me. During some years, I trained with her for 25 hours per week. Not only was she an amazing coach in the gym, but she ended up acting like a big sister to me, coaching me through hard life lessons and holding me while I cried. It was evident that she genuinely cared for all her athletes. My family was going through some challenging times, and Angie took me in and cared for me like we were family. She was always a strong figure in my life; I looked up to her and loved being around her. Now, years later, to see her on this path of healing is no surprise.

Angie has always been deeply intuitive, empathic, and nurturing. She has been a true angel in my life, along with countless others. It only makes sense for her to continue healing and sharing her gifts."

"Love fearlessly, time and time again. There's no better feeling in the world."

~ **Dr. Kristina Engel, D.TC.M.**

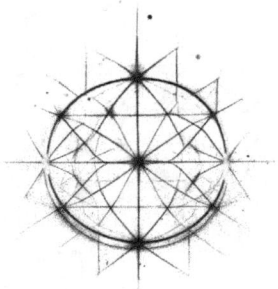

APPENDIX

What follows isn't another chapter in the arc of this book, but a sacred testimony. Kristina walked beside me in this medicine, and through the four elements, she threads her own story of remembering and rising.

I chose to place her words here, in the Appendix, because they're not meant to explain shamanic leadership but to embody it. May her witness remind you this path is lived, breathed, and carried in community.

THE SACRED HEART OF SISTERHOOD

Journey Through Belonging, Boundaries, and Becoming

Kristina Skye

The first time I met Angel, it felt less like an introduction and more like recognition. Something in her eyes reflected a part of my own spirit—a familiarity that whispered, *Ah, here you are.* That moment planted a seed, one that grew across two decades into a living sisterhood.

I first encountered her through the world of gymnastics. At the time, I sat on the board of directors for my children's club, and we were in a season of upheaval. The club needed a new location, and with only one coach left, we clung to a fragile vision of rebuilding. Our coach assured us she had a plan.

"If only I can convince my old national-level coach to join us, everything will fall into place," she said with conviction.

Angie's so great. You'll see. Don't worry, I'll convince her.

Eventually, she did.

I remember walking into our new location for the first time and finding Angel there alone, assessing the space. She moved through the space with authority, already commanding its possibilities. She didn't just enter the gym; she claimed it. There was a presence about her, a steadiness that made me pause. At that moment, I had no idea this club was her baby; she birthed it years before and now stood in the place of its rebirth. All I knew was something powerful arrived, and I felt it in my bones.

About a month into the season, Angel surprised me with flowers and a card. On the front was a picture of a horse for her, and a cat for me. Inside it read: *We're more alike than we're different.* It was a simple gesture, but it marked the beginning of a recognition between us. She saw something in me that resonated with her own spirit, and in that moment, the threads of sisterhood began to weave themselves quietly between us.

Later, I came to see how fitting those animal symbols were. The horse—a creature of strength, freedom, and forward motion—mirrored Angel's commanding presence and her drive to reclaim and rebuild what she once created. The cat—independent, intuitive, and quietly powerful— mirrored my own way of moving in the world, more subtle but no less sure. At first glance, horse and cat may seem unlikely companions, yet together they reflect a balance of power and presence, instinct and intuition. The card was more than a kindness; it was an omen. We were, indeed, more alike than different.

What I couldn't yet see was the true beginning of a sisterhood. At first, it was simply admiration—her strength, her vision, her way of taking up space with certainty. But over time, that admiration softened into resonance. We were different in many ways, yet something in her mirrored me back to myself. She reflected a kind of leadership I only began to name within my own life: fierce yet compassionate, structured yet deeply intuitive.

Sisterhood doesn't announce itself with a title or a role. It reveals itself slowly, through trust built in quiet moments, through trials weathered side by side, through the silent knowing that someone sees you—truly sees you—and chooses to stay. That day in the gym wasn't just about the future of the club. It was about the future of a relationship that became a compass for my own path of leadership and service.

INVOCATION OF THE DIRECTIONS

And so, before I share our journey through the Four Directions, I pause to honor them here:

I turn to the *east,* where new beginnings rise with the morning light, and I honor the spark of recognition that first drew us together.

I turn to the *south,* where fire warms and trust grows, and I honor the laughter, the learning, and the vulnerability we shared.

I turn to the *west,* where shadows lengthen with the setting sun, and I honor the endings we faced, the trials we endured, and the healing that followed.

I turn to the *north,* where wisdom gathers like stones on the Earth, and I honor the lessons harvested and the service born of our bond.

And at the *center,* I honor the heart—the circle of sisterhood that is both anchor and compass, guiding me to lead with authenticity and love.

EAST – THE BEGINNING

In the east, the sun rises, and everything is bathed in possibility. It's the direction of vision, of clarity, of the first spark that calls us forward. Looking back, the east was already at work in those first months with Angel. Something new was beginning, though I couldn't yet name it.

Our relationship started in the shared space of the gym, but even then, it carried a current beyond schedules and strategy. Angel's presence was luminous; she could walk into a room and shift its energy without saying a word. I found myself both drawn to her strength and softened by her generosity. That balance made me pause. She wasn't just leading with authority; she was leading with heart.

The east reminds us that leadership begins not with performance, but with presence. It begins with seeing clearly; both the vision of what might be, and the truth of what already is. Angel carried a vision for the gym long before I understood its roots. What she saw wasn't just walls and equipment; she saw potential, legacy, and renewal. Standing beside her, I was invited to see more deeply, too—to widen my own vision and recognize the sacred ground we stepped onto together.

And it was instant. There was a pull. There was a knowing. There was a remembering. From the very beginning, we found ways to spend time together—hours on the phone, long days at the gym, even late nights connecting through online video games. We became close very quickly, drawn together by a force that felt beyond our choosing. Boundaries often blurred, and soon we knew every intimate detail of each other's lives. It was as if the east flung open a doorway, and both of us stepped through without hesitation.

At that time, my toxic marriage was wearing me down. Angel could see it in me. She knew the story all too well: the exhaustion, the control, the subtle cruelties that leave you questioning your worth. She'd been there before. She recognized the signs because she lived them. I was her mirror. She wanted me to leave, to choose myself, but I wasn't ready.

And then one day, the mirror turned. I looked at her and pointed out that her marriage wasn't really any different from mine. She saw my truth, and now I reflected hers back to her. That was the nature of our bond from the beginning: we held up mirrors for one another, sometimes lovingly, sometimes painfully, but always with the unspoken agreement that the truth mattered more than comfort.

This is the gift of the east: the light of clarity. When the sun rises, it exposes everything—the beauty and the brokenness alike. In Angel's presence, I could no longer hide from my reality. And in mine, neither could she.

But the east brought more than truth; it also brought awakening. This was when the door to spirituality opened for me, and we stepped through it together. At first, it was simple things: pulling angel cards, holding crystals, lighting candles, experimenting with small rituals. But those little practices carried big meaning; they were acts of remembrance, breadcrumbs leading us back to the sacred.

We began to speak about the deeper truths we always carried but rarely shared: our long-held spiritual beliefs, our questions, our unshaped longings. These were the most vulnerable parts of ourselves, the pieces you risk revealing only to someone who feels safe enough to hold them. And so, we walked this new path hand-in-hand, like two toddlers finding their footing, discovering the ground beneath us was holy.

The east taught me that beginnings aren't always gentle. Sometimes the first light reveals truths we'd rather not see, and yet that clarity is the gift that sets us free. In Angel, I found both a mirror and a companion: someone who could call out the illusions I lived under, and someone willing to let me do the same for her. That mutual seeing was the foundation of our sisterhood.

The east also taught me that every path of leadership begins with awakening.

Before strategy, before service, before performance, there's presence. There's vision. There's a willingness to open the door to something new, even if you don't yet understand where it will lead. For me, that door was spirituality. With Angel, I stepped through it tentatively at first, guided by simple practices and brave conversations. But the act of stepping through together was itself an initiation into a new way of being.

This is what the east asks of us as leaders: to be willing to see clearly, to name what's true, and to walk through the doorway of awakening even if our legs tremble, for in that first light the seeds of transformation are sown.

SOUTH - TRUST AND PLAY

If the east was about awakening, the south was about learning to stay awake. It is the place of fire—of warmth, passion, and play. In the south, our bond grew roots, not only in truth-telling but also in the everyday intimacy of laughter, trust, and shared experience.

Angel and I spent hours together, and the boundary between friendship and family blurred in the best possible way. We laughed until our sides ached, told stories until the early hours, and found comfort in simply being together. There was a childlike joy in our connection, as if some long-forgotten part of us received permission to play again.

But the south is also the place of vulnerability. Fire not only warms; it also burns. In our closeness, we risked exposing the most tender parts of ourselves: fears, wounds, desires, the private truths many keep hidden. We built trust not by avoiding the flames, but by daring to step closer to them together. And while that fire refined us, it also carried within it the promise of trials yet to come—shadows that would one day test the strength of our bond.

As the years unfolded, the south's fire burned away what no longer served us. Circumstances changed, as they always do in life. Both Angel and I left toxic marriages and navigated new beginnings at nearly the same time. She moved to Cranbrook to carve out a new start, while I began university in Calgary as a single mother of four. Though our paths diverged in geography, they ran parallel in spirit. We each stood at the threshold of reinvention—fragile, hopeful, and brave all at once.

We put many kilometers on our vehicles in those years as the five-hour drive between us became a familiar journey. There was no meeting halfway; one of us always made the full drive. That stretch of highway became a thread weaving us together, proof that distance couldn't diminish what we built. Whether through celebrations, crises, or ordinary days that simply needed sharing, we kept showing up for one another. The road itself became a kind of ritual, carrying our sisterhood back and forth like a heartbeat.

It didn't really matter what we did when we got together. The point was being in one another's presence, where we could be completely present. In her presence, I found comfort and understanding, a deep sense of belonging. In our differences, we found sameness. We shared a passion, a deep desire to move forward and expand. We shared a love for exploring our spiritual paths, for learning and growing together. We even shared a love for road trips and cantaloupe.

I remember one particular road trip where we set off, and our conversation and laughter were so intoxicating that it was only after an hour of travel that we realized we had gone in the complete opposite direction from the one we intended. This was the magic of many of our adventures: the joy was never in the destination but in the journey itself.

Those years were marked by growth. Individually, we learned who we were outside the confines of unhealthy relationships. Together, our sisterhood evolved into something even deeper: a sanctuary where we could show up raw and unguarded, knowing the other wouldn't look away.

The south taught me love, laughter, and belonging are as essential to leadership as vision and clarity. It reminded me fire not only burns away what's false, but also warms what's true. In Angel's presence, I experienced what it meant to be fully seen and fully accepted—not because of what I could achieve, but because of who I was. That kind of trust creates a space where growth isn't forced; it unfolds naturally.

Leadership, like sisterhood, is sustained by presence. It's not always about the grand plans or perfect strategies, but about showing up — making the long drive, sharing a simple meal, or laughing so hard you lose track of the road. These seemingly ordinary moments are what build extraordinary bonds.

In the south, I learned joy isn't separate from the spiritual path but woven into it. Play is a form of prayer. Vulnerability is a form of courage. Belonging is a form of power. And when we nurture these qualities in our relationships, we carry their warmth outward into the world, leading not through fear or control, but through trust, love, and authenticity.

WEST - SHADOWS AND TRIALS

If the south was fire in its warmth, the west was fire in its shadow. This is the direction of water, of endings, of descent into the places we would rather not go. Where the south gave us belonging and joy, the west asked us to face loss, grief, and the unraveling that comes before transformation.

No sisterhood—no matter how full of laughter and light—can remain untouched by the shadows. For Angel and me, this was the season when the flames we played so close to began to scorch. The same closeness that gave us comfort also meant there was nowhere to hide. Old wounds surfaced, patterns repeated, and trials came that tested whether the bond we built could withstand the darkness.

In the mirror, we also see our shadow. When we dance too close to the fire, we risk getting burned. And burned we got. As our bond became closer and closer, and our lives became even more inextricably intertwined, the burns became inevitable. Boundaries blurred, and as we struggled to juggle our individual identities, the very closeness that once kept us so alive began to feel like the thread threatening to unravel all we had built.

We began to feel the sharp wounds of boundaries crossed too many times. The small things turned into big things. Obstacles we once traversed with ease became insurmountable. Mixed messages, friendships taken for granted, our lives became so very tangled that there was no way to separate them.

At first, we tried to carry on as though nothing had changed, but the tension grew heavier with every conversation. Words once received as laughter now landed as criticism. Silence, which was once comfort, began to feel like distance. It was as though the language we built between us suddenly turned foreign, and neither of us could remember the grammar of closeness.

And then, like glass striking stone, our sisterhood shattered. Once cherished and carefully orchestrated, it smashed into a thousand fine pieces. There seemed to be no way forward. Even if we could glue the pieces back together, how could anything ever be the same again? This fracture left a wound inside me so deep that I felt I would never be whole again. It carried with it the heavy ache of abandonment—the fear that I didn't only lose her but also lost a part of myself that only existed in her presence.

The west doesn't allow illusions to stand. It asks us to look directly at what we'd rather turn away from. For us, this meant confronting the shadows within ourselves and our relationship with the same honesty we once used to call out the shadows in our marriages. But seeing our own reflection in another can be far more painful than pointing to it from a distance.

The west taught me every descent is a kind of initiation. To be broken isn't failure; it's the doorway to transformation. Yet in the moment, all I could feel was the ache of absence, the hollow space where our bond lived, the raw sting of abandonment, the despair of believing nothing could ever be whole again.

But the wisdom of the west is this: death and endings aren't the end of the story. They're the compost of the soul, breaking down what was so something new may grow. The grief I carried wasn't wasted. It became the soil in which deeper truths one day took root—truths about boundaries, about resilience, about the courage it takes to let go when holding on only deepens the wound.

Leadership, like sisterhood, can't be all light. To lead with authenticity is to walk through the shadow places; to face loss, betrayal, and endings; and to allow them to carve wisdom into your being. The west demanded I confront not only the fracture in our relationship, but also the illusions I held about myself. In dark descent, I began to understand even the deepest wound carries the potential to become a source of strength.

NORTH - WISDOM AND SERVICE

If the west is the place of endings, the north is the place of harvest. It's the direction of earth, of grounding, of wisdom gathered through experience. Where the west stripped me bare, the north offered a slower, steadier path of integration. In its stillness, I gathered the pieces of myself that remained and listened for what I could carry forward.

The fracture of our sisterhood left me hollow, but in that hollow space a new kind of strength took root. The north doesn't rush. It invites patience. It teaches that wisdom isn't born in a single moment of revelation, but through the steady work of reflection and integration. With time, I began to see that even the pain had a purpose. The fire of the south and the shadows of the west refined me; now the north asked me to carry that refinement into the world as service.

Our reconnection began slowly, softly. Time passed. There was space between us, and we filled that space with mutual respect, compassion, and understanding. There was a new awareness around what had been and what could be. The physical distance was greater this time and proved to be the necessary buffer in rebuilding our relationship. Our sisterhood was reborn through the ashes.

We supported each other from a distance at first, taking tentative steps forward—video chats scheduled, carefully seeking approval and consent as we crept forward. We learned all over again. What stayed the same was that gentle knowing: the knowing that the foundation we started to build so long ago would hold this time.

In the north, our bond matured into something that could flow outward. What we once held just between us began to radiate into our families, our communities, and our work. Together, we found ways to mentor others, to co-create, and to build spaces where authenticity and belonging could thrive. The lessons of our bond, collaboration over competition, service over self, presence over performance, became teachings we could embody in the wider circles of our lives.

Our sisterhood was solidified through a group trip to Mexico, a shamanic journey facilitated by Angel herself. That trip tested us more than we ever could have imagined, pushing us to our edges and asking us to surrender to something larger than both of us.

In Teotihuacán, I came face-to-face with some of my deepest fears. The intensity of that experience shook me, and in that vulnerable place, Angel was the one who held me when nobody else could. Her presence became my anchor, her steadiness the ground beneath me. That moment etched itself into my soul as a reminder of the sacredness of sisterhood, the way it holds when everything else falls away.

Angel, too, had life-altering experiences on that trip, moments that cracked her open to a transformation still unfolding. And just as she had held me, I supported her through the upheaval of her own rebirth. Together, in that ancient place of pyramids and prayer, our paths converged once more. The bond that was fractured and reforged was now tempered by fire, shadow, and grace—unbreakable, because it was remade in truth.

The north taught me wisdom isn't gathered in isolation, but through relationships. Through the courage to fall apart and the grace to come back together again. It showed me leadership ripens when we allow our experiences, both joyful and painful, to be harvested as medicine not just for ourselves, but for others.

That trip to Teotihuacán was pivotal for us both. It sealed what was broken, transformed what was tested, and reminded me that sisterhood isn't about avoiding struggle, but about walking each other through it. In holding one another through fear, grief, and rebirth, we discovered the essence of service: to witness, to support, and to remain present even when the path is uncertain.

The north asks us to gather the wisdom of our journey and offer it back to the world. For me, this meant carrying forward the truth that collaboration is stronger than competition, that service outlasts performance, and that leadership grounded in love will always create belonging. From the ashes of endings, we sow the seeds of service—and in the circle of sisterhood, we share every harvest.

CENTER - INTEGRATION

At the center of the circle is the heart. Here, all directions meet, and here, our sisterhood ultimately rests. The east gave us vision and awakening. The south gave us joy, trust, and the fire of belonging. The west stripped us bare in shadow and endings. The north offered harvest, wisdom, and service. And at the center, I see none of these can exist in isolation. They belong to each other, just as Angel and I belong to the circle we walked together.

Our sisterhood has not been perfect, nor has it been easy. It's real. It's alive. It's sacred. From our first spark of recognition to the fire of our laughter, from the shattering of our bond to the rebirth that followed, every step shaped me into the leader I'm becoming.

The center reminds me sisterhood isn't only for the two who share it; it ripples outward. The love and truth exchanged in one relationship become medicine for every circle it touches. When we dare to show up fully for one another—to witness, to challenge, to celebrate, and to hold steady through the storm—we create a bond that teaches the world what authentic leadership looks like.

For those seeking to embody this energy in their own relationships, the center offers these lessons:

- **See and be seen.** Allow yourself to be mirrored in both your light and your shadow.

- **Honor presence over perfection.** It's not what you do together, but the depth of how you show up that matters.

- **Let joy and play be sacred.** Laughter is as holy as prayer.

- **Hold each other through endings as well as beginnings.** Sisterhood deepens when we remain, even when it hurts.

- **Share the harvest.** Let the wisdom you cultivate together flow outward into service, family, and community.

At the center, I remember leadership isn't about standing above others but standing with them. It's about weaving belonging through the simple but radical act of staying present—present to the spark, to the joy, to the shadow, and to the wisdom.

The circle is unbroken. And as I stand at its center, I carry forward the knowing that sisterhood—in all its laughter, its trials, its wisdom, and its grace—is itself a form of shamanic leadership, authentic strategy, and service beyond performance.

BLESSING OF THE FOUR DIRECTIONS

To the *east,* I call the first light. May you rise each day with clear vision, and may every new beginning awaken your spirit to truth.

To the *south,* I call the fire. May warmth and laughter fill your circle, and may trust burn bright enough to carry you through both play and vulnerability.

To the *west,* I call the waters. May you find the courage to face your shadows, to grieve what must be released, and to let endings wash you clean for what's yet to come.

To the *north,* I call the Earth. May wisdom take root in your being, and may every harvest of joy and sorrow become nourishment for the world you serve.

And to the center, I call the heart. May you remember you're never alone. May sisterhood, in all its fierce love and tender grace, be your anchor and your compass, guiding you always home.

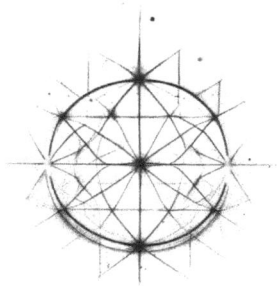

ANGEL GOLD
POWER JOURNEYS AND WORKSHOPS

Angel experiences living in the mystery as part of her daily life.

As she continues to walk with one foot in one world and the other here on earth, she now shares her magic and medicine with others throughout their community and across the world.

She chooses to do retreats, as we know, the powerful transformation that happens in sacred sites. Experiencing initiations in a group setting and allowing the mystery to dissolve your limited beliefs while you are out of your normal routine expands your consciousness in the most incredible way. She is a guide. Not a hand holder. She provides the container for you to do your inner work. There is no better way to grow and expand than through the presence of others, in sacred ceremony, on sacred land.

Join Angel on her next adventure:
https://www.angelgold.ca

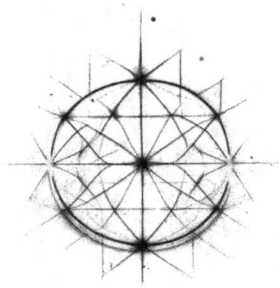

WELCOME TO FIRE HEART MYSTERY SCHOOL

FIRE HEART MYSTERY SCHOOL

A living temple for the wild, the sovereign, and the seekers of soul.

Here, myth meets medicine. This is not a place for surface fixes or spiritual performance. It's where your fire is honored, your truth is sharpened, and your power is reclaimed.

You will be asked to go deep:

- into silence

- into story

- into the edges you've been avoiding

And you won't go alone. You'll be held in a circle, where remembrance is fierce and belonging is real.

We walk with animal medicine.

We weave ritual, dreamwork, shadow work, and sacred leadership.

Each step is infused with Toltec and Andean wisdom, crystal magic, breathwork, and elemental ceremony, woven together with a high-performance mindset.

This journey is for you if you're ready to show up as the fearless warrior and powerful goddess that you are. If you're done being a victim in your own story, ready to break out of the programming you've carried since birth, and willing to do the work at the deepest level possible.

It's not for those waiting to be rescued, ruled by fear, or unwilling to claim their own power.

Step into the Fire Heart Mystery School, and you step into the untamed: intuition awakened, boundaries fortified, and leadership lived from bone marrow.

In the mountains of Peru, I was gifted the Incan name **Nina Songo** by Quero Shamans - *Fire Heart.*

This medicine has been birthed through the fires of my own initiation.

https://www.skool.com/fire-heart-mystery-school

Solar Hugs and Sparkly Blessings,

Angel Gold

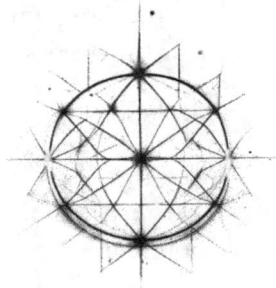

ADDITIONAL PROGRAMS

Fire Heart Breathwork

Reiki, Usui System of Natural Healing Certifications

Private Healing Sessions

Dreaming Ceremonies

Digital Programs

www.angelgold.ca

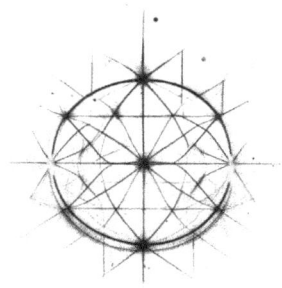

ACKNOWLEDGMENTS

I would like to express special gratitude to my many teachers who walked this path alongside me.

All humans we encounter have teachings for us. I acknowledge and appreciate the following humans for directing their attention toward me, committing to a path of love, and shining their light to help me see clearly, with unconditional love.

Jorge Luis Delgado, Brandon Raynor, Terry Masson, James Wedmore, Lee McCormick, Miguel Ruiz Sr., Jose Ruiz, Miguel Ruiz Jr., and HeatherAsh Amara.

Yes, to this constellation of light that created this container—I'm forever grateful for all these souls who said yes to this polarizing ride into the depths of shamanic leadership.

Thank you to Wilbur Tate and Kelly vdH - Kaschula for sharing their gifts of visionary art for the graphics and design, and bringing this medicinal work of art into a light-coded treasure. One that would not have existed without the love and support from Laura DiFranco. Not only has she been an amazing publisher to work with, but a fierce partner and friend who believed in me. This book wouldn't exist without her direction and superpowered support of me and my mission. I am so grateful for our team of experts in their field.

Which brings me to these beloved authors that said yes to this mission: Thank you to the *Shamanic Leadership* authors: Laura Di Franco,

Jorge Delgado, Eliza James, Kristina Skye, Grace Solaris, Emoke Molnar, Rachelle Golding, Dustin Kaiser, April Kaiser, Spencer MacDonald, Emily Atlantis Wolf, Daphne Paras, Grace Kohn, Sharla Duncan, and Bradford W. Tilden.

I would also like to thank our parents and friends who have walked beside us. Those who cheered us on, challenged us, and reflected our shadows with love. Every soul who enters our story brings medicine: some teach us how to rise, others remind us how to soften, and all, in their own way, shape who we become.

Since my previous book was birthed, life has continued to school me in boundaries, the quiet art of self-trust, and razor-sharp discernment. The lessons haven't always been gentle, but they have been sacred. For every teacher, every mirror, every moment that revealed more truth than comfort, I am grateful.

YOUR WILL REQUIRES YOUR DISCIPLINE AS YOU MASTER
A NEW WAY OF LIFE.

~ANGEL GOLD

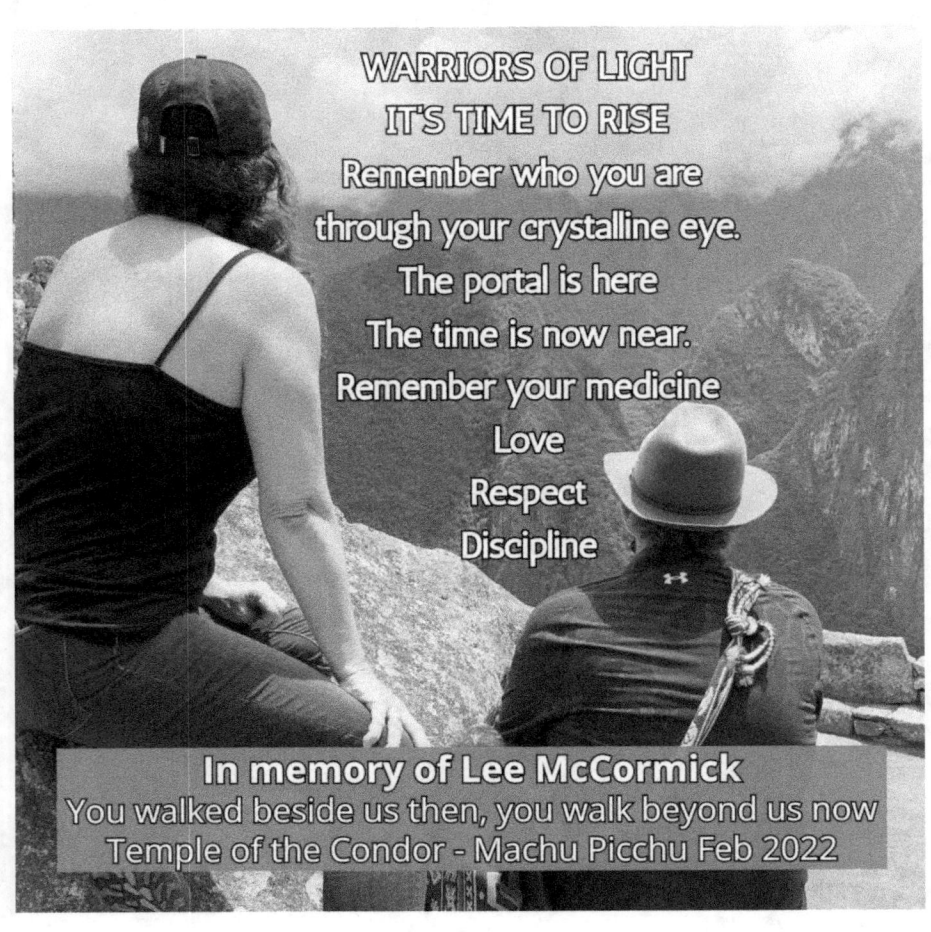